NEWLY REVISED!

HOW TO SET YOUR FEES AND GET THEM

Filled with information and examples on how to charge the right rates for your services.

KATE KELLY

HOW TO SET YOUR FEES
AND GET THEM
by
Kate Kelly

Fifth Edition 1994

Copyright © 1994, 1989, 1986, 1982 by Kate Kelly

All rights reserved.

Published by
Visibility Enterprises
Six Oak Avenue
Larchmont, NY 10538

International Standard Book Number:
0-9603740-2-7

Printed in the United States of America

www.howtosetyourfees.com

TABLE OF CONTENTS

"How do I know what to charge?"

Of all the questions that plague business owners and professionals, this one seems to head the list. Even for those who have been in business for quite some time, the question reappears in a different form: "They didn't blink an eye when I told them my fee. I bet they would have paid more."

This book is written for everyone who spends time worrying about how they charge. You may be newly self-employed and curious about some of the basics of pricing, or you may have been in business long enough to have encountered a wide variety of difficult pricing dilemmas. Whatever your field and experience, I think you'll find the advice and information contained in this book helpful.

I'm a free-lance writer and consultant, and I originally started looking into this subject because I was having difficulty knowing what and how to charge for my writing. Whenever it came to quoting a client a price, I felt uncertain and found many excuses to under-price myself: "I'm not really sure what my time is worth..." "I've never done this type of work

before..." "I don't know what the competition is getting..."
"They probably don't have a very big budget for this..." "I'll
bid a little low because I don't want to lose the job..."

I hated feeling like that—and I didn't like working for less
than I needed to, so I decided to research this topic the way
I would a project undertaken for a client. I'd learn what there
was to know about it, and then I would be better able to handle
the business end of my business.

What have I learned? That setting your fees is both a skill
and an art. It's an art in that every situation is different.
Sometimes negotiations will go smoothly and you'll get what
you want; other times, the client will have unrealistic expectations, and you may need to do some artful negotiation to
emerge with what is a fair deal for you.

But setting fees is also a skill, which by definition means that
it's something that can be learned. You don't have to have
a gigantic ego to feel comfortable charging several hundred
dollars a day for your services! If you know a few formulas
which most business owners use and have the confidence the
advice in this book can give you, then you, too, can master
it.

I can't promise that you'll always get top dollar for any future
work you do. There are too many variables in any business
negotiation to be assured of that. What I can promise is that
by reading this book you'll attain a feeling of mastery and
confidence, and a much greater degree of comfort when faced
with the task of setting your fees.

www.howtosetyourfees.com

I. WHAT ARE YOUR TIME
AND KNOWLEDGE WORTH?

Most people starting out don't even have a general idea of
how to charge. And those who have been in business for a
while are usually looking for better ways of doing it. What's
the best way to set a fair rate? Our first task is to determine
what your time and knowledge are worth in the market place.

A Formula for Estimating Your Rate

If you're just starting out, the first figure you need for
estimating your rate is the annual salary of someone who does
your job full-time in a staff position. (If you already have
an hourly fee, skip ahead to the next section, "What's the
Going Rate?")

Are you (or were you) or do you know someone currently on staff performing tasks similar to those you want to do? For example, are you a marketing manager who wants to become an independent marketing consultant? Or are you a graphic artist who wants to go free-lance? If so, then there is a mathematical formula that will give you a rough estimate of what you need to charge. If there are no staff jobs comparable to what you want to do—for example, calligraphy or starting a home organizing business—then skip to the next section: "What's the Going Rate?")

If you're not currently employed in the type of work you plan to do free-lance, you can get an annual salary figure from someone you know or by consulting appropriate compensation surveys available through many trade associations. Or visit the business section of your local library and take a look at the salary ranges given in the federal government's *Occupational Outlook Handbook*; in addition, the librarian should also be able to provide you with salary updates put out by the Bureau of Labor Statistics.

Let's suppose that you're making $32,000 per year on staff. That means you earn approximately $615 per week ($32,000 divided by 52 weeks); $123 per day ($615 divided by 5 days); and $15 per hour ($123 divided by 8 hours).

To arrive at a starting figure for your hourly rate once you are self-employed, **multiply $15 by 2.5**, some even say 2.8 or 3. That brings you to $37.50 per hour for an initial per-hour estimate. Since $37.50 is a rather cumbersome number, you may want to round that up to $40 or down to $35, and later we'll discuss how to decide whether to round up or down.

That's quite a difference, getting $37.50 instead of $15.00...
Are you that much better just because you're self-employed?
Perhaps (!) but the true reason for the multiple figure is
overhead. The staff artist usually doesn't pay for a complete
medical plan out of his own pocket, and business operating
costs and the employer's part of social security are all
covered by the company. He also doesn't have to worry
about "down" time. As any self-employed person will tell
you, it is a rare occasion (and a *very* long work week) when
you are able to put in forty billable hours for a seven-day
period. (There are 21 weekdays in most months, and you
should expect to bill out for only 15 of them.) Part of any
professional's time must be spent on administrative details
and marketing, and of course, vacation, holidays, and possible sick leave must be accounted for, too. And *that's* what
the extra hourly pay helps cover. It also helps compensate
for the lack of a guaranteed weekly check which anyone on
staff receives.

Now take your own figures and put them into the following
formula:

Hourly Pay x 2.5 = Hourly Rate for the Self-Employed

But wait--there's still more research to do.

What's the Going Rate?

How does the rate you have determined compare with what
the market will bear in your community? You will almost
always find that fees for services vary depending on the
locale. Prices in major cities will usually differ from prices

in more rural areas, though sometimes the price difference may surprise you. If a certain type of expertise is in high demand in a certain area, then the fees those professionals can command will usually be higher. For example, for a time, physical therapists were in short supply in parts of Georgia. As a result, physical therapists there were earning a higher hourly rate than they would have had they been in a major east coast city!

The best way to research this is to *check the competition.* In some professions, the self-employed who compete with one another have banded together for friendly networking to compare notes, share information, and generally support one another. Here in New York, "round tables" of specific groups of professionals (designers, accountants, free-lance editors, etc.) meet frequently; several of the career counselors in the city talk regularly to compare experiences; there has been nationwide linking of professional organizers; and the American Society of Journalists and Authors is an example of a formalized group which serves this purpose for writers. You may also find helpful networks on an on-line computer service. Look around for ways that you might locate other professionals and benefit from their pricing experiences.

If you find there is no formal network, start watching for industry surveys about what is charged. You may find that someone else has done some of the research for you. If not, then you'll need to continue researching. Look for others offering services similar to yours and call and introduce yourself. As you talk, you may learn what the going rate is and how they describe their fees—a day rate, an hourly fee, etc.

Of course, in some fields the competition may not be so agreeable. Then talk to the types of people who would be potential clients. Find out what they have paid for similar services in the past.

Once you know the general rate for services in your field, you will be able to adjust your fees accordingly. You may find that the figure derived from the 2.5 formula is a bit high or a bit low for your market. If so, you can make the necessary adjustment. If you're just starting out and need to attract business, then a lower price than the competition may be just the edge you need. If you find that you're charging less and have enough business then you'll probably want to raise your fees to be more in line with everyone else. If you're charging more and are getting all the business you need, then terrific. You must be worth it.

Does Your Rate Cover Costs?

Let's suppose you have determined that you can charge $50 per hour. That may sound terrific, but if in addition to other expenses, you rent an expensive office and support a staff person, you may not be able to cover the bills even with that hourly figure. Here's how to be sure your hourly rate really covers costs.

When it comes to expenses, the self-employed have two types of costs: *direct* and *indirect*. *Direct costs* are those incurred while working for a specific client (these might include travel, messenger, postage, printing, etc.) These costs are generally passed through to the client, and we'll discuss this more fully in Chapter VIII.

Indirect costs are your overhead—general expenses such as rent, insurance, taxes, social security, professional services, office supplies, utilities, and so on. These expenses are simply the cost of doing business.

Right now we want to look at indirect expenses. Go to your records to come up with a figure for your annual indirect expenses. If you are just starting a business, estimate what your annual expenses will be. Certainly you must have a figure for rent and insurance and a pretty good guess as to what utilities will run. When it comes to taxes, remember that you'll pay taxes on gross revenue after expenses are subtracted.

Next, you need to know how many billable hours you work in an average week. As we've discussed, no self-employed person can bill out 100 percent of the workday. Factors such as personal efficiency and steady clientele contribute to how much time is billable—the accounting firm which primarily works for two or three steady clients can invest less time in marketing and sales calls than if it needed a regular supply of new customers; and the well-organized person who has had a lot of experience will be able to bill out more of the average workday than can the person who is just getting started and must research each phase of most jobs. In general, most professionals find that 50 to 75 percent of their time is billable, with the remainder being spent on marketing and administration.

If you do not know how many billable hours you have in the work week, use your office calendar or use the daily time sheet provided (see Appendix) to start keeping accurate records of how you spend your time. Note time spent on client projects as well as the time spent on general office details and marketing.   In a couple of months, you should be able to determine what percentage of your time is actually spent working for clients and how much of it is spent on marketing and running your business.

Once you have a figure for your direct costs and another for your billable hours, you'll be able to work through the formula below.

For a moment refer back to the previous formula.   Let's suppose that you have determined that on staff, you would be making $12 per hour. Twelve dollars times 2.5 (the multiple given in that formula) brings your estimated hourly rate to $30 per hour.

Now we need to check the validity of this rate.   Let's now suppose that your annual *indirect* cost (overhead) is $16,000, and that you can bill out an average of 25 hours per week. This means you have 1,250 billable hours per year (25 hours per week times 50—assuming you allow two weeks for vacation).   Your overhead ($16,000) divided by your billable hours (1,250) determines the amount you need to make per hour in order to cover indirect costs ($12.80).   Add to that the cost of your labor (the amount you would be paid in a staff job—$12), and that brings you to $24.80, leaving $5.20 (approximately 17.5 percent) of the hourly fee for profit. Business people generally hope to make a 20 percent profit, so you are close to a very workable figure.

Here is the formula again, for you to work through with your own figures:

1. **Billable hours/week x 50 weeks/year = billable hours/year**

2. **Annual indirect costs (overhead) divided by billable hours/year = hourly costs**

3. **Hourly costs + hourly pay + 20 percent profit = hourly rate**

Once you have a final figure, you can make some decisions. If you find that you've been able to keep costs low (say $8 per hour), and your hourly labor ($12) plus hourly costs ($8) leaves you a full $10 (or about 33 percent) of the $30 fee for profit—wonderful. If you're able to get as much work as you like charging $30 per hour then you can enjoy the large profit margin. Or you may decide this is a good opportunity to upgrade your office or equipment. Or if times are a bit lean and you'd like more work, you'll know that you can afford to temporarily drop your hourly rate to see if that brings in more business. (When lowering your rate under these circumstances, present your new fee as a "special offer." That way, when business picks up, you can easily slip back to your higher rate by simply dropping the special offer.)

If, however, your costs tip the scale on the heavy side (say $16 per hour), leaving you only $2 of the $30 fee for profit ($12 labor costs + $16 expenses = $28), you have reason for concern. Raising your hourly rate is one possibility, but if you've done your homework then the $30 figure you selected was chosen partly because that seemed like what the

market would bear. If you go much above that, you may
meet price resistance. The other answer is to lower your
expenses. Or perhaps the solution lies somewhere inbe-
tween. You might bring some costs down and raise your rates
slightly in order to come up with a figure that makes for a
healthier business. Experiment a bit on paper to see what is
feasible, and if you decide you must raise rates, refer to
Chapter XIV for hints on how to do it without losing customers.

Checking this formula at the end of the year or whenever you
have a change in pricing or in your expenses will help you
keep tabs on your profit margin and improve your long-term
profitability.

A Double Standard?

There may sometimes be situations when having two rates
makes sense. If you feel that you could get one price from
one segment of your market (or for one aspect of your
services), but not quite that much otherwise, then simply
structure your fees accordingly.

Graphic artists are an example of professionals who differ-
entiate between their services. The design concept work is
a challenging part of the work where quality of work will
vary from person to person, so an artist may charge a high
rate (perhaps $50 an hour) for the more creative design work
and a lower fee (perhaps $35) for the time he or she spends
actually laying out the agreed-upon design. (Eventually an
artist may build business to the point that he or she can hire
someone else to do the layout work so that more of the artist's
time can be billed at the higher design-concept rate.)

Some business owners raise their hourly rate for certain types of consultation work. One woman who owns a direct mail marketing company has one set of fees for the creative work of producing mail-order pieces for the client, but she sets a higher hourly rate for client consultations concerning other marketing ideas. "My fees for the direct mail pieces are competitive with others in the business, so I don't want to change them," she explains. "However, the marketing advice I can offer has been gleaned through many years in the business, and it's important to me that I'm well-paid for the consultation time."

Some entrepreneurs, especially those in unusual businesses, are often approached by people wanting advice on how to start similar businesses. While they sometimes choose not to consult with people who would be directly competitive, most generally don't mind spending some time—paid for, of course—offering advice to a person in a different geographical area or market. For this type of service, any business owner should charge above their regular hourly fee. After all, the advice being offered has taken months and years to acquire.

You might also think in terms of rewarding certain clients. If one particular customer buys a major chunk of your time, then you might consider billing that account at a slightly lower rate—a discount for continuing business. (Some also use this system to reward old customers, giving them a slightly lower price than new ones.) Don't be too generous though. While volume discounts make sense in manufacturing where volume usually reduces production costs, this isn't true when what you're selling is time.

If you're considering using more than one price for services, keep these thoughts in mind:

- The best method for establishing some variation in prices is by treating aspects of your business as different products you market. Straight consultation time is one price; consultation with a final report is another, etc. This permits people to hire you for what they can afford. Otherwise, consider volume (of time) discounts to reward larger clients. You can also give discounts for payment in advance.

- Don't make it too complicated. You don't want a lower price for one client to come back to haunt you: "But you only charged so-and-so $x...." Your rebuttal must always be that the services provided under those circumstances were substantially different.

- Professionals in counseling fields sometimes vary their charges on an ability-to-pay basis. However, you must use a standardized rate for everyone when a third-party (an insurance company) contributes part of the payment.

- For worthy causes, you may want to establish a "Robin Hood" system that allows you to donate your services or charge them at cost.

II. CHOOSING THE RIGHT FEE STRUCTURE

In certain professions there is a "norm" for how to state your fee. For example, most people seeking therapy know they'll be paying on a per-visit (basically per-hour) basis; clients seeking legal advice also know that their bill will be computed based on an hourly fee. Yet if you're hiring a decorator, his or her fee is often set as a percentage of the goods purchased.

However, for most, deciding how to present your rate to the client falls into the realm of the great unknown. If you tell a potential client what you charge per hour, will they faint? Or not hire you? If you price by the project, how do you make sure it doesn't take up more time than you've allotted? How does charging "per person" work? There are many different variables, and this section will discuss your best options.

(If you have employees, read this chapter and then refer to Chapter XV, "Billing for Staff Members," for additional information.)

Per Hour

Since every self-employed professional should know his or her hourly worth, this may seem like a logical way to present the facts to the client. However, there are both pluses and minuses to using this system.

When does an hourly rate work well? If yours is the type of business where you perform your job on site, then the hourly system may be perfect for you. Organizational consultants who must perform their duties on site or who are expected to attend a good number of company meetings frequently use a per-hour or a per-day rate.

Along with on-site consultants, others who have made the hourly rate work well are speakers who quote an hourly rate for a specific presentation. In this type of situation, the number of hours billable to the client would be only the hours actually spent on-site doing the presentation. One home economist who frequently does cooking demonstrations points out that she must be certain the hourly rate quoted is high enough to also pay her for the time spent in advance preparing the food to be demonstrated.

One note: If you do present your fee in per-hour terms, you may want to adjust it based on what "sounds" right. One consultant says that he found that $50 per hour caused clients difficulty because they viewed it as "half a hundred" and could quickly do the arithmetic to calculate what their likely total cost would be.   "For some odd reason, once I moved my fee to $70 clients seemed to find it much more palatable," he notes.

However, there are three key ingredients that are helpful in making per-hour system work. The first is keeping careful track of your time. You can use the old method of noting times on your calendar or on a client time sheet (see Appendix), but computers are now equipped to keep track of billable time and can even generate your invoice from the raw data you enter. Visit your local software store and ask about time-sheet programs. A good one will record your time with a built-in stopwatch, calculate and log the hours, and monitor time and expense budgets. Aids such as this are getting better and better, so you'll likely find something that is just right for your needs.

The second ingredient for making the per-hour method work is some sort of reassurance that your *client is accustomed to working with outside professionals who earn a respectable hourly rate*. In conversation, you will likely pick up a sense of their experience with hiring outsiders. If this is the first time they've hired anyone but an office temporary on an hourly basis, then look for another way to quote them your fee. Why? Those who are unaccustomed to hiring from the outside are more likely to be judgmental, and they may think: "Gee, at my salary level, I make only $25 per hour... Why is this person charging $45?" Unaccustomed to consultants' typical fees, they don't consider that outside consultants must pay for items such as overhead, social security, and medical benefits (extras most staffers take for granted but which at many companies are valued at about one-third of one's annual salary). Because they are trying to compare apples (staff salary) to oranges (your fee as a free-lance), you will almost certainly suffer. With clients such as this, you will fare better quoting a project rate (discussed later), where your hourly fee can be disguised.

The third important ingredient in using an hourly rate is being able to *establish some sort of a cap or limit on the project.* In this case, one must sympathize with the client. No one likes looking into a bottomless pit, especially with an open checkbook. Will a project take you ten hours or 100 hours at $25 per hour? There's quite a difference between $250 and $2500.

Capping the project can be as simple as telling them you'll do ten hours work and wait for a project review and their "okay" before you proceed, or it could consist of some sort of agreed-upon deadline. If they want the work finished within three days, then both of you know there will be a limit to the number of billable hours you can accrue.

The proprietor of an information-on-demand research service finds the hourly system with a cap helpful when a client has limited funds and/or the scope of the project is difficult to estimate. She sometimes proposes doing a few hours of initial research before taking the project any further. (This may give her time to complete the task, or it may simply take her far enough to be able to tell the client how many more hours of work will be involved.) That way she and the client can discuss how to proceed. However, by starting with a capped hourly arrangement, the client knows from the beginning exactly how much the initial research is going to cost.

Another consultant, whose business involves detailed and extensive analyses of major companies, works similarly. Initially he sells a client forty billable hours at the end of which they receive a report which offers some concrete conclusions as well as a prescription for work that could still be done. "They like the fact that they get a report, and if they choose to stop there, then they've still gained from our time and effort," he notes. "However, most clients continue with my recommendations, and because I've been inside the company long enough to see the broad picture, I am generally able to present them with a project price or a very good estimate of the number of days the remaining work will take."

Per Day

Presenting a per-day rate offers most of the same advantages and disadvantages as the per-hour rate. As a matter of fact, management consultants will find that companies are far more likely to talk in terms of "per day" rather than "per hour." And most consultants bill for at least a half-day even if the work took only an hour, so there are definite advantages.

Some business owners quote an hourly rate, and then offer a slight discount for a full day, for example, $20 an hour or $145 a day—$20 times eight hours would be $160, so the client would receive a $15 discount for buying a full day's time. The benefit to you is being able to sell a full eight hours of one day. If you had to have eight separate clients in order to bill those eight hours, then factoring in transportation and transition time, it would probably take a minimum of two days to work one hour for eight separate clients, and that doesn't even factor in the time spent finding and developing eight different people for whom you could work!

As with the per-hour method, setting a limit on the time you expect a particular assignment to take can often make the difference between getting the job or not.

If your on-site work requires advance preparation or the tailoring of your materials to the needs of that particular corporation, be sure to bill accordingly. One writing consultant who commands $600 per day stresses that his fee actually must cover what amounts to more than one day's work since he must spend a couple of hours preparing for each company. However, his $600 fee, he feels, compensates him for this.

Per Project

In many cases, a per-hour or per-day rate may needlessly expose you to discussions of exactly why you charge a much as you do. (Remember that many staff people are uncomfortable with the fact that a consultant or free-lancer may make more per hour than they do.) You may find that burying your per-hour rate in a project price increases the likelihood of getting the job: You provide the client with a set price, and then he or she can evaluate whether or not accomplishing the project is worth that amount of money.

No customer would buy a suit if the store said, "Fine. We'll let you know what it costs once we see how many hours it takes our tailor to make it..." By the same token, people are less likely to hire when they are in the dark as to what the ultimate bill will be. The project price solves this problem by removing the unknown. Perhaps a good rule of thumb is that if a portion of your work for a job will be accomplished off the premises of the client company (so they won't have any idea how much time it takes anyway), you might do well to quote them a project fee. While a client might gladly pay $2000 for a specific assignment, he might cringe if he realized he was paying you $100 an hour.

Like almost all of the rate structures we've discussed (with the exception of the straight, uncapped hourly rate), there is risk involved. The art here is in getting very good at your estimates. If you bid $1000 on a job where you hope to make approximately $30 an hour, then you can't afford to work much more than 30-35 hours at the job. How can you guarantee that you'll be able to bring it in at that?

With experience—and a good record-keeping system—you'll soon be a pro.

The first thing you need is a system for learning about your own work habits and pace. Like attorneys who must record the hours (and quarter-hours) they devote to clients so that the law firm will know how to bill, you, too, must get in the habit of recording exactly how much time you spend doing what. You may find it helpful to establish time sheets for each project, or purchase appropriate software for your computer. Keep track of time worked on a specific day, expenses incurred (postage, transportation, copying, etc.), phone calls made and what was accomplished (contacts made, research done, ideas generated, etc.)—everything you would need for a final billing or to substantiate your efforts on the client's behalf. (See Appendix for a sample worksheet.)

Or your record-keeping system could be as simple as making notes on your business calendar or in your computerized date book system. Keep track of time worked for different clients each day as well as time spent on administrative details. The record of time spent on in-house management will help you evaluate the use of your time, staffing needs, and any work flow problems you encounter.

At the end of each month, tabulate and review how your time was spent. A final review at the end of the year will show you how your hours were allotted in relation to the goals you intended to accomplish. It will also provide you with a "time history" for various types of work. You'll soon learn that a certain type of project almost always takes a similar number of hours. When you bid on that type of job again, you'll have a very good way to estimate how many hours the project will take, and therefore, how much you need to charge.

And what if the project is very complex? Many on-site interviews combined with several progress reports and a detailed analysis at the end... How do you estimate it?

Every job can be broken down into small parts. How many interviews will be involved? (If you are uncertain, discuss an estimated number with your client and in your agreement provide that if the interviews go substantially above that number then it will affect your fee.) Estimate a length of time for each interview, and then factor in any other research that will be involved. Add additional time for the progress reports. Add still more time for interim discussions with the client. Factor in travel time for visits to the site and allow for thinking time as well as writing time. Add all these figures together, and then inflate your figure by several hours—jobs always take longer than you expect.

Working to fit the fee can be an important advantage of the per-project quote and helps solve what to do about the old adage: "The client doesn't know what he wants until after he sees what he doesn't want." If you sense that the client doesn't really have a good understanding of what he wants, then prepare a preliminary piece (sketch, rough draft, initial plan, etc.), investing as little time as possible. That way you can spend the bulk of your time on the project after the client has had the opportunity to focus on what he or she really does want.

By the same token, if a client has volunteered that he has only "x" number of dollars allotted to a project, you can evaluate whether you can make that fee worth your time. If you're a financial planner, then perhaps you can't undertake a complete investment advisory program for the client, but maybe you could help establish a family savings plan. If you know what the fee is going to be, you may still be able to work within it.

If something goes wrong with a project and you have to devote more time than expected, be sure to evaluate what happened. Did the client misrepresent the work involved? Did he require more hand-holding than you anticipated? Was the task an unfamiliar one, causing you to do more background work than you expected? Once you know why, it will be easier to avoid it the next time.

Per Piece

Illustrators, calligraphers, or people providing word processing services are a few of the types of businesses where a
per-piece billing system is sometimes used.

To calculate a per-piece cost, you simply determine how
much time it will take to type an average page (word-processing business) or to provide a certain type of illustration
(illustrator) or document (calligrapher), and take into account
the time spent. For example, if an average letter takes a
word-processor about 15 minutes, then the per-letter cost
would be one-quarter your hourly rate; an illustration that
generally takes five hours would be five times the hourly rate,
etc.

Like all pricing systems that mask your hourly rate, the
per-piece method helps you avoid a discussion of time spent
on the job. With complicated illustrations or elaborate calligraphy, this can be a benefit in setting a fair price. The
drawback is on smaller items: a calligrapher's client may
question paying several dollars per envelope, or the customer
of a word processing firm may balk at the steepness of a
per-letter rate. For these situations, a project rate may serve
you better.

Since the word processing industry has grown out of typing
services where per-piece billing is the norm, this is an area
ripe for some pricing creativity. A woman who runs a word
processing service recently attended a lecture I gave, and
afterwards, we discussed the difficulty clients have with

paying a fair per-piece rate for "a simple business letter." (They quickly forget that the person providing them with the typed letter has probably struggled with poor handwriting, corrected punctuation, and can store the letter on disk in case any similar letter ever needs to be sent.) The business owner was having difficulty covering her overhead and didn't think she could command a high enough per-piece rate to make ends meet. I suggested a new strategy. Why not ask customers to put her on a monthly retainer for which her firm would cover assorted secretarial duties for the month? For the business that needed only a few letters and some miscellaneous work done each month, the fee could be $20-40 while businesses with greater needs would pay more. That way she could make her fee more palatable to the client by burying the per-letter charge in a lump sum. (See below for additional information on handling a retainer agreement.) In making this type of an arrangement, it would be vital to create a letter of agreement that thoroughly spelled out what was to be covered for the basic retainer and what would cost extra. A per-hour rate for work above and beyond the monthly allotment should be specified.

Per Person

You might encounter—or suggest—a per-person rate structure if you were presenting a program for a group of company employees, or if you were the speaker at a professional meeting or a community event. In essence, it is really just another way of presenting the rate you need to receive per hour.

It, too, offers certain benefits. One consultant feels that corporations like the "neatness" of a per-person package because they can make their plans without worrying about the clock (as they might if you bill on a time basis). She also points out that $75-$100 per employee is a small per-head cost for a company, yet if it requires only a few hours of your time, a small group can quickly add up to an impressive sum! If you were to charge just $50 a head for a six-hour one-day workshop, then with only 20 people you would earn $1000 for that day.

The consultant continues: "Doing an effective workshop for twenty people is more effort than doing it for fifteen, because you have more individuals whose needs you must address. If I billed on an hourly basis, then I would receive no extra compensation for my extra effort. With a per-head fee I do."

To establish your per-person rate, you need to decide how much money you want for the time involved. (Your figure should also take into account any expenses you would have in providing materials or samples, etc.) Then try to get a rough estimate of how many people they think might attend.

A corporation can probably estimate within a head or two and reliably deliver as promised. If you are speaking before the membership of a professional group, they will probably only be able to approximate. To protect yourself in either case, insist upon a guarantee. Let's supposed that for a speech before a community organization, you would like to earn between $100-$400. The group estimates that forty people will attend, and they have agreed to pay you $10 per person. Under these circumstances, you might request a minimum guarantee of $100 (or ten people). It's a gamble. You may walk away with the minimum of $100, or if more than forty come, you'll be glad you charged per person. If the organization is charging for the evening's program, this method also provides them with a system that is fair. If they have light attendance, they aren't stuck trying to pay an exorbitant fee.

You might also consider the per-head rate for a secondary billing system. I once taught a course where I was guaranteed a flat fee of $250 for a lecture, but if more than ten people came, I was paid an additional per-person fee. This helped compensate me for the money I spent on extra course materials and for the mental wear and tear of offering personalized advice to so many individuals. (Course materials could also be billed as a direct expense. See Chapter VIII.)

Flat Rates for Specific Services

Just as doctors charge one price for looking in your child's ear and another price for swabbing the back of the throat for signs of strep, some businesses lend themselves to a fee for service system.

If you are selling the same service again and again, a flat fee makes a lot of sense. You will have a good idea of the time commitment it generally takes, and as a side benefit, having a set price serves as a good marketing tool. Friends tell friends about your service, and because they can cite a set price, the referrals that come to you should quickly convert into additional sales.

Who uses flat rates? Anyone who offers a type of service that can be repeated without that much variation in time spent. One counselor who uses flat rates offers a consultation service which can be accomplished in two sessions. A written evaluation is part of the package, and a flat fee covers both sessions as well as the evaluation. "It takes a little more time with some clients than others, but on the whole it averages out," she says. "I find that the advantage of being able to quote one price to customers far outweighs any possible disadvantages. They like knowing exactly what their cost is going to be."

Attorneys sometimes use a flat rate for preparing wills, partly because they can make a good estimate of the time each document will take, and partly because—even if they suffer a small loss—it's a good way to introduce new clients to their practice.

If you opt to use this system and offer several different services you perform, print up a price list. It validates your pricing method and makes it seem less negotiable. It is also a fair method for the consumer. They know exactly what they are paying for and exactly what they are getting. One attorney who specializes in working for small businesses drew up a list of the types of legal services any entrepreneur planning to incorporate might need. After each item on the list, he offered a range of the costs involved, leaving himself some leeway to charge more for a complicated job or a nettlesome client. In addition, the list reminded the client of all the legal matters that would need to be taken care of in the process of incorporating (thereby enhancing the attorney's chances of getting to perform the additional tasks for the client), and it provided the client with a general range of what the costs would be. This type of price list could be drawn up for many types of businesses and could function as a sales tool (by presenting them with a full range of the services you offer), as well as a way to educate potential clients as to what is involved and what the costs may be.

Retainer Fees

A retainer is an agreement between client and consultant specifying that a set fee will be paid at regular intervals (usually monthly) in return for agreed-upon services. For a client the benefit of a retainer is that they have formed a relationship with—and can count on availability of—an expert professional whose services they may need. The benefit to the consultant is regular income and stability. Essentially, there are two types of retainer agreements:

1) The most common type of retainer basically serves to put you "on staff" for a specific period of time—it might be one day per month, or it could be three weeks each month. The agreement would outline specific tasks to do or goals to reach and you would be expected to work toward them during the allotted time. Whether the work is done in your office or theirs, and whether you are to do the work on specific days or at your convenience usually depends on the nature of the job.

2) Less frequently, a company may need a certain professional's services irregularly, but because they want easy access to someone who understands the nature of their work, they pay a retainer simply to maintain that relationship. If they don't use the services during a particular month, fine, and if they do, then the professional would give the client the specified amount of time. Ideally, there

should be no accrual system—time not used in one month would *not* be carried over, but this should be clarified. Obviously, it would be very difficult for a consultant to suddenly find he owes and must "pay" a client a month's worth of days.

Your retainer fee would, of course, be based on your regular rates. If the client wants you available at least two days a month, then your retainer fee would be set accordingly; that is, for two days time, it would be approximately twice your daily rate.

In advance, *agree upon the rate of pay for any additional work done.* Some months the client may need you for longer than the stipulated amount of time, and your letter of agreement might specify: "Any work performed that is above and beyond what is described above will be billed at the hourly rate of _____."

If you have never before worked with a particular client, request a three-month trial period under which to test out the details of the retainer agreement. Consultants are often so excited at the thought of solidifying one or two relationships (so that less time must be devoted to finding new clients), that they are overly eager when they enter into some retainer agreements. What if you sign on for a year and then discover that your price is below what you're worth to them? Or what if you learn that you just can't stand the people? For these reasons, I recommend that if you have not yet worked with a client, start slowly. That way both client and consultant can try out the relationship without signing on for a long-term commitment. At the end of three months, you may decide that no amount of money is worth putting up with them; or you may want to revise your retainer fee upward in order to be more fairly compensated for the time you are spending on their needs. Or perhaps the original agreement was just perfect—then sign with them for a year!

Contingency Fees

Contingency fees are known by a variety of terms, but they all have in common a basic element: payment is made only if the project is successful. *If* a lawyer working on contingency wins the case, he gets paid; *if* a magazine likes an article written on speculation, the writer gets paid; *if* a sale of a product (anything from a car or a home to a life insurance policy) is made, then the salesperson is paid.

Here are some of the situations where contingency fees are common:

If high stakes are involved. In lawsuits concerning plane crashes, personal injury, product recall or medical malpractice, attorneys frequently work on contingency. In return for the risk they take in possibly not being paid at all, they generally command a large percentage of the money received by the claimant if the case is won.

Professionals advising in the start-up of new businesses will sometimes work on contingency as well. For their services, the professional might take a small percentage ownership in the company. If the business is successful, they do very nicely. If the business flops, they earn little or nothing.

If you are in sales. In sales, commissions—a payment based on the percentage of the sale that is made—are the norm.

Whether you sell stocks, houses, insurance or refrigerators, you are likely to be working at least partially on a commission basis.

If you are in placement. Employment agencies and executive recruiters often work on a contingency basis. If they find the right candidate for a specific job, they are paid an agreed-upon fee by the company. If no placement is made, there is no fee.

If you are asked to work on speculation. Writers are sometimes asked to work "on spec" which means they are to prepare a piece for submission with not guarantee of payment. If the publication likes it, a sale is made; if they don't, there is no payment at all. Though writers usually do not have to work on this basis, sometimes it's the only way to break into a new market.

Two other reasons people sometimes work on contingency include:

1) For the experience. If you have been unable to convince a potential client that you could overcome your lack of directly applicable experience and handle his job, then perhaps a contingency arrangement might be suggested. You get the experience you want, and the client pays you only if you succeed.

2) To fill in during a slow period. If you've hit a lull and no one has expressed interest in hiring you under any circumstances, then you might consider proposing a contingency fee.

Confidence is probably the single most important ingredient to being comfortable with a contingency arrangement. If you think you can make it work out, then it may be worth giving it a try.

In the first edition of this book, written a dozen years ago, I warned strongly against the use of contingency fees. Today, however, the business world is changing, and businesses that formerly operated on project or day-rate billing methods are using contingency fees as a way to sell their services very profitably. The change has come about when clients began balking at flat or time-based rates.

One new situation where contingency fees are used are businesses that have evolved to help other businesses cut costs. A good number of consultants have gone into business to help clients untangle the confusion over all the various telephone service options. Typically, they'll come into a client's office, evaluate the system, and recommend modifications (or a new system) guaranteed to save the client money.

After ten years in the consulting business, one communications consultant turned to the contingency system when the economy forced his company into it, and to his surprise, it has worked out well. They have structured their business so they take 50 percent of the first years savings (their competition takes a smaller percentage but over 5 years time). To get money in advance, they estimate the amount they expect to be able to save the client and ask for that as an upfront fee to have operating money.

Another consultant takes 10-20 percent of the yearly operating-cost savings (for three years) that he realizes for steel mills. With the scope of his business, he only needs one client every two to three years.

One entrepreneur came up with a variation on the contingency fee which both encourages people to try her somewhat novel service while still rewarding her in a way that she felt was fair. Specializing in stock certificate research, she charges a flat fee (under $100) for researching the status of any stock certificate a customer brings her. If the certificate has value, then her firm retains 30 percent of the first $2000 recovered and 20 percent of any value above that. If her research turns up nothing, then she refunds the entire research fee.

One caveat: Avoid any sort of situation where the results you produce must be left to subjective judgment. For example, a publicist working on contingency or a per-placement (of publicity) basis either will or will not get the article placement she seeks for the client. If there are results, they can be clearly defined. However, a researcher asked to look into a subject for "helpful" information will have a problem. No matter what information is found, the client can always declare it as "not helpful" to avoid making payment.

If you enter into a contingency agreement, consider both the risks and the rewards, and if you proceed, *define the terms clearly and in your favor*.

Percentage Fees

Most contingency systems go hand in hand with percentage-fee systems. A literary agent sells a book to a publisher and takes a percentage; a real estate agent sells a home and takes a percentage of the sale price; a consultant saves a company money by establishing a more efficient system for the business... In all these cases, both agent and person represented benefit from increasing the level of the sale—sell the movie script at the highest price, sell the house at the highest price, save the company more money... everyone is happy.

Most industries have a standard practice for the percentage charged, and the professional in question has to attempt to work to fit the anticipated fee—or make up for hours lost on one project by bringing in a larger profit on another.

However, percentage fee systems have also been used in areas where it didn't always make sense for the customer. For example, though you can now find architects who will prepare plans for a flat fee or on an hourly basis, many still bill by charging a percentage of an overall construction project. The problem with this system is that the more expensive the job, the greater the compensation. Or in the decorating field where a percentage fee is often charged, the more expensive the couch the greater the fee netted by the decorator. Consumers are becoming wary of such arrangements. It also isn't ideal for the professional—it fails to financially reward the consultant who works hard to save a client money.

For this reason, some consultants are switching to other pricing methods. Some architects and decorator/designers are offering hourly or project rates, with only a portion of the payment coming through a percentage billing. Some are even agreeing to cap the total amount of income realized through the percentage system in order to allay client concerns about running up costs on the project in order to run up his or her fee.

Another change has come about in major accident and liability lawsuits. Lawyers have been criticized for the percentage fee system when their are astronomical awards. As a result, some are coming up with a sliding scale—generally 33.3 percent on most cases, with a sliding scale that goes down as the award goes up. This is regulated in some states; done voluntary elsewhere, largely due to public criticism. No one liked the situations where the accident victim is faced with a life in a wheelchair, and the attorney who wins the large settlement walks off with several million dollars in fees. While the attorney should certainly be well-compensated, it becomes problematic when the percentage amount becomes an amount most people won't see in a lifetime.

In Trade

Occasionally, it may occur to you or to the client that each of you could be of service to the other. A dentist might barter with an accountant or an interior decorator might trade services with a calligrapher.

The value of services rendered are to be reported as income for tax purposes, but if you can work out mutually beneficial services, it is likely to be a favorable arrangement for both of you.

Handle payment in trade the way you would any other business arrangement. Define beforehand the exact rates for the services to be traded, and set a time limit for "payment."

You may want to give a full year for trade of services, or you may not want to extend it for longer than a month. While these arrangements are generally made verbally, it is a wise business practice to start putting them in writing. Things do go wrong--even among friends.

Summary

Here's a summation of the benefits and drawbacks of the fee structures discussed:

Per Hour

- Good for work done on site.

- Good way to start a project while becoming acquainted with the work at hand.

- Place a cap or limit on a job, if the client hesitates.

- Disadvantage: Client may balk at hourly rate, since it includes your overhead, etc.

Per Day

- Good for on-site work.

- Corporations tend to prefer per day to per hour.

- You may need to build in preparation time if your per-day fee covers only work done on site, i.e., a workshop.

- Disadvantage: Client may balk at rate.

Per Project

- Only you know exactly how you arrived at the figure. Client need not know hourly rate, yet client has exact figure he can count on.

- Good when part of job is being done off-premises.

- Offers the opportunity of working to fit the fee or tailoring a job to suit the client's budget.

- Disadvantage: You have to become very good at making estimates. (With time, you will.)

Per Piece

- Allows you to place a price tag on your work which may make it more marketable. For example, the publisher knows exactly what ten illustration will cost, and therefore, he or she feels more comfortable with commissioning the artist to do the work.

- If calculated properly, the method works well for both parties. The entrepreneur is fairly compensated for the work, and the client knows in advance how much something will cost.

- Disadvantage: Clients may balk at a per-piece cost on smaller items where the price may sound steep. Here, the project rate will likely serve you better.

Per Person

- Where applicable, the per-person method provides an alternative to hourly or daily rate.

- Offers nice "package" rate for corporations or community or professional groups.

- Rewards you for large attendance.

- Disadvantage: Even with a built-in minimum, you run the risk of low attendance and hence a lower fee.

Flat Rates for Specific Services

- Good when you are selling similar services over and over again.

- Consumers like it because they know exactly what they will pay.

- Aids in building word-of-mouth that will easily convert into additional sales.

- Disadvantage: Only applicable when you sell a standard service.

Retainer Fees

- Combines the advantage of steady income with the pleasures of being self-employed.

- Requires clear agreement about time commitment for the fee.

- Disadvantage: Unwise to jump into a retainer agreement until you've had time to get to know the client. Offer to work on a project or per-day basis (or, initially, set a three-month limit on the retainer) until you are comfortable enough with the work and the client that you feel you can set a fair fee for a long-term agreement.

Contingency Fees

- This is the "norm" in fields such as sales and placement, and is being used increasingly by different types of businesses.

- Disadvantage: You might not get paid at all. If your field of work does not usually have contingency agreements, then it's probably more risk than you need to bear. Always avoid a contingency fee if a subjective judgement of performance will be involved.

Percentage Fees

- Standard practice in some industries.

- Provides opportunities for shared success in fields such as sales.

- Disadvantage: In fields such as architecture and design, it rewards big spending, so customers are resisting. Some professionals are switching away from percentage-fee systems or are using it in combination with other billing methods.

In Trade

- Can be of mutual benefit to both parties.

- Must be reported as income for tax purposes.

- Handle as any other business agreement, agreeing upon prices and time limit for trade.

- Disadvantage: If the professional you're trading with isn't that good, then you've lost more than you've gained. Better to hire the best you can afford.

III. DECIDING WHAT TO CHARGE

We now need to consider the best way to handle an early
"fees" discussion with a potential client. We will assume that
they are interested in what you have to offer (either because
they have approached you with a specific need or because you
have done a first-rate job of convincing them of the value of
your services). They're going to want to talk money—possibly earlier than you want to.

Have Time On Your Side

When it comes to giving a price, most people just want to
blurt out a figure—almost any figure—just to get past the
awkwardness of the discussion.

The problem with this is that it leaves them in a weak position
when it comes to being paid what they are worth.

It's important to be *psychologically ready to discuss your price*. You must believe in yourself, and believe that the terms you are offering are fair ones. It's also important that you not act under pressure. Take a deep breath and realize that you *can* take the time you need.

In some discussions, money will be broached immediately, before you've even seen the material involved, in which case you're certainly not prepared to quote a fee! Other times, the client may have called you in for a meeting where you've seen the work and met the team with whom you'll be working.

In almost all cases, *no matter when the subject of money comes up, make it a practice to get back to them later.* Unless you're simply quoting an hourly or daily rate which you've set in advance, or unless you're giving them a fee in a proposal you've written (in which case you've met with them previously and had ample time to consider how much work is involved), then it's too early to talk money.

You need to go back to your office and evaluate the time and the expenses involved, or it will be difficult to quote a figure that will be fair to both you and the client. Insist that this is the best way to handle it, and promise to call them within a day or two (or even an hour will give you some breathing room): "I need to go over the figures and the project again before giving you a price. If I quote you a fee now it wouldn't be fair to either of us, so I'll call you tomorrow (or after lunch or in an hour) with the costs involved."

This maneuver provides you with the opportunity to shift gears. During the meeting with the client, any consultant is in a "sell" mode. When you're trying to convince a client to give you the job, it is a poor time to also try to put a price on your head—your price will inevitably be set to please them, not you. Do everything you can to get out of their office and call back later with the price. And if this is a new type of undertaking, it gives you the opportunity to make a few phone calls to further research what a fair fee for the project would be.

While all this sounds good in theory, I know that there are times when you get backed into a corner—I've been there. I remember a telephone conversation with a very desperate potential client who rarely uses free-lancers. She was eager to hire me, but—more importantly, she claimed—she had to get permission from her boss to go to the outside at all. I had not seen the material she had described, and it was 10 p.m. on a Friday night—a poor time to do business. She made it very clear that the job wouldn't be farmed out to a free-lancer (me) unless she could call her boss and give him a rough idea of the cost. I really wanted the job, and since I felt trapped, I gave her what I stressed was a "ballpark figure." A mistake.

The next morning when I saw the material, I realized there was more work involved than she had indicated. I mentioned this and gave her a figure 25 percent higher than my first estimate. She coolly announced that her boss had approved the ballpark figure but stipulated that she was to pay no more.

The moral of the story is that though I got the assignment—which was indeed important to me—I ended up working for less than what I should have been paid. I learned. I should have taken the gamble that she and her boss could have made their decision *after* I saw the work involved.

Despite this warning, there will almost surely be times when you must discuss money sooner than you might like. Those jobs will probably carry consequences—in my case, it was being locked into the initial figure I gave. If you feel you must proceed, *quote high.* You will almost certainly encounter the unexpected.

But in most cases, you don't have to quote a fee on the spot. Try to remind yourself that there's no rush. Feeling that you have time on your side will make you more comfortable with the figure you quote.

See The Materials First Hand

How many times have you had a potential client say, "Oh, there are just a few things for you to do—it won't take any time at all." Or: "All the research is done. You won't have any problem."

If you've ever had that happen, then you know the true story. The "few things" could be a major overhaul of a department. And "all the research" could be two pages of notes with the comment, "Oh, well, I guess the rest is in my head."

Before you quote your fee, be sure to arrange to see the materials with which you'll be working or the problem you are to solve. If they want you to set up a new organizational chart, ask for the current one and ask questions about their problems with it. If you are to design a new corporate logo, find out what they dislike about the current one. Take a look at the employee manual that needs to be re-written.

For the same reason, you'll also want to meet the people with whom you'll work. Do they seem well-organized? Are they pleasant? Do they agree with your approach? What is the staff like? They can speed a job along or hinder it's progress, so you'll need to evaluate them as well.

Also consider: Who will make the final decisions? While it's fine to gather information from a committee, it is very important that your final directive come from a single individual. It's impossible to satisfy a team of bosses, so you shouldn't even try.

Establish Exactly What The Job Is

Another important part of early meetings with the client is to *define the job*. Exactly what is to be accomplished? Where does the job begin? Where does it end?

Defining the job is particularly important in fields such as public relations where the results cannot be guaranteed. While you can provide them with a press release, you cannot guarantee them front-page coverage in the local newspaper.

How extensively will your work be used? Is the new personnel system you're developing going to be used by one store or twenty? If the answer is twenty, your fee should be higher. The project will likely be more complex because of the expanded usage, but it's also important to keep your fee in line with the program's value.

In businesses such as photography, illustration, or graphic arts, where and how will what you produce be used? For in-house materials, your fee would be lower than something produced to appear in a national ad campaign. And what about rights? If what you produce can only be used by that client, then your task is simply to price the job based on time spent and value to the company. However, if the design or photograph is something which might be sold again under other circumstances, then it's important to negotiate rights. Many pros choose to sell first-time rights only; others specify unlimited rights to the work for a limited period of time (e.g., one year). If the client insists on a buy-out, then your fee should be higher than if the rights revert to you at some point. Even then, you can generally negotiate for the right to display the work in your portfolio.

Writers must also be concerned about rights. This is very important in the publishing industry, but it can be significant when selling to the corporate world as well. While you needn't worry about retaining rights on a company brochure, if you are writing a secretarial how-to manual (something you might market elsewhere), you may want to charge a little less and retain the rights or provide that the rights revert to you under certain circumstances (cessation of publication; sale of the company, etc.) Selling limited rights might also be appropriate if contributing a generic piece to an in-house publication.

Writers and artists of all types should also always specify the number of revisions covered by the fee.

This is also a good time to *educate the client*. Take the time now to explain the reality of what can be accomplished and what can't. You should also tell the client a little about how you operate. An educated client will place higher value on your services (and pay for it!), and they will be more accommodating in the relationship if they understand the true nature of the job.

While no one relishes doing a written proposal, it's an excellent way of outlining the job for the client, and it provides you with the opportunity to put down on paper all that you anticipate the job will entail.

*****

If this were an actual situation and you followed these steps to place a price on your services, then we're getting very close to the point where you ought to know what your fee is going to be. To recap:

1) You've given yourself breathing room to stop and carefully evaluate what you want to charge.

2) You've seen the material you'll be working with and met the people.

3) You've defined exactly what it is you're going to do for the client and educated them as to the possible and the impossible.

What Costs Extra

Before coming up with a final figure, you'll want to factor in what I call the "extra" considerations. These are the picky little problems which can cost you time and money. Consider:

Travel Time: How far away is the client? How many trips will you have to make? If you're going to be spending 45 minutes to an hour or more in transit, then it's likely that every time you must visit the client, you'll lose the better part of a day. If you visit them once or twice, you needn't be concerned, but if you'll be making many trips, you need to charge for it. It's billable time that is unavailable to you to sell elsewhere.

The same principle applies to air or long-distance car travel. You're perfectly justified in billing your day rate for travel time as you are losing a day in the office. Many who consult all day and fly home that evening, also bill a half-day for the evening travel time. For particularly long flights, request flying first-class. The company may have a policy against it, but it's worth a try.

Holidays: Often outsiders are called in to help out on weekends or holidays when the company's staff is unavailable. If you work over a holiday, you deserve more.

Tight Deadlines: You may also have been hired because the company needed the work "yesterday." They've slipped up on the deadline or they are anxious to finish a project, so they push hard for you to deliver. If you'll be working under a lot of pressure and/or if doing the project will mean setting aside other things you're working on in order to make their project your priority, then that, too, should cost more.

Special Qualifications: Whether you are a lawyer, a Ph.D., or an M.S.W. you may have the educational qualifications that a client needs—or *must* have in someone doing the job. And advanced degrees aren't the only kind of expertise clients may need to pay for. Perhaps you have a great track record for launching new products or maybe you're the only person in the state who is familiar with a certain type of insurance claim—that background is something the client should pay for because they aren't going to find it in just any consultant.

Special Expertise: What if, when you see the material they are providing, you realize that they have badly misrepresented the back-up materials they promised you? If your own resources (personal library, specialized knowledge, access to people, etc.) are vital to the project, then charge more.

The Pain-in-the-Neck Factor: Face it. Some people are very difficult to work with. They keep calling to check on you, or they can't make up their mind what they want. Or they may simply need hand-holding and constant reassurance that this is the right thing to do. Build in the extra time this may take so that you don't feel taken advantage of in the end.

The Go-Between: Sometimes you'll end up with a job where the project is the brainchild of the V.P. of the department, but his or her assistant is "going to be working with you." Be wary. The intent of the vice president is wise delegation. For the outside consultant, the result may be lack of clarity. The "go-between" may decide that pages three and four of your report need to be rewritten; the boss may feel the problems lie with seven and eight. In other words, you can end up correcting the flaws spotted by the go-between only to discover that those "flaws" weren't a problem at all. If you can't arrange to work directly with the person whose opinion will rule, then build in extra time to compensate for that. A note regarding your relationship with the go-between: Sometimes these people feel threatened by an outsider. Anything you can do to allay his or her concerns may be helpful in creating a better relationship.

Uniqueness: Does the market perceive you as a one-and-only? Are you the author of a "hot" book? Are you a well-known artist? Are you an attorney who has just won a major case? If you are perceived as unique, charge for it.

How Much Are the "Extras" Worth?

As much--or as little--as you want. Here's how to figure it:

First, you must consider how badly you need the work. If things are going well, why subject yourself to difficult working conditions unless they are willing to pay for it? However, if it's been a little too quiet lately, then your first priority is probably to turn in a bid that will get you the job. By charging too much for extras, you run the risk of pricing yourself out of the market.

Next, evaluate how much bother a particular "extra" is to you. If a job requires that you have to work over the Fourth of July and you didn't have plans anyway, then you may be more interested in picking up the fee than in billing them extra. However, if it means you must work over the Christmas holidays, and you'll be missing out on a lot of the fun, then you'll probably want to be well rewarded for it.

How much can you ask? To decide that figure you have to come up with a number that will reward you for your trouble without putting your overall fee so high hat you lose the job. Sometimes you may feel that an extra $100 is all that you can afford to ask. Another time, you may feel that the agony of the job is going to be so great that it isn't worth it unless they pay you a hefty sum. If that's the way you feel, go for it! There are plenty of consultants who have been well-compensated for work on which they set a very high price.

Playing for the Advantage

Like a high-stakes poker game, it's to your advantage not to have to play the first card. If you can get a hint of what's in the client's hand first, you'll play your own cards with more confidence.

One piece of information that is important to have is knowing whose idea the project is. If a senior level person is behind the project, then you know that it will be treated with respect and will likely be followed through to completion. If the idea came from someone lower on the management ladder, then the project isn't necessarily doomed, but it may run into more snags along the way.

Next, try asking, *"What's the budget for this?"* That all-important question can sometimes switch the negotiating advantage in your favor. The client may decide not to answer it, but it won't hurt to have asked.

While the budget may have to include other expenses besides your fee, it still gives you a quick glimpse as to what kind of money is going into the overall project. If the figure is high, then you know you can be quite fair to yourself. If the figure is a low one, then if you really want the job, you'd better adjust your fee to bare bones.

On the occasion when they do discuss the budget with you, you'll be glad you remembered that it "never hurts to ask." And suppose they go right ahead with this line of thinking and tell you what they intend to pay you. Even if you're thrilled with the price, wait a beat. If they really want you, they may increase it immediately, fearing that their offer wasn't enough.

If the amount offered as your fee is scandalously low, then you'll have to reply: "I'm afraid I can't do it for that amount, but let's see what we can do." Then keep reading. Maybe there's still a way you can do business together.

What Does the Client WANT to Pay?

Of course, what we really wish is that we could read the client's mind. What do they expect to pay? What do they think of you vs. the others? Are you going to get the job anyway, or do you have stiff competition?

One comforting thought you might hold is that far more often than you would think, the client has no idea what to make of you. Many staffers rarely hire outsiders, and yet when they do, they're pretty desperate. For that reason. they want to like you (or like one of you, if you're among several vying for one job), and they know less than you do about what the job should cost. One corporate vice president told me, "The first time I hired a free-lance writer, I had no idea what the going rate was so I was willing to pay whatever she said."

Another executive mentioned: "I'm really surprised at how low some of the rates are. I would expect to pay more."

Just as you have no published price list that tells you what to bill, they have no corporate manual that tells them what to pay.   Unless you're dealing with someone who regularly hires from the outside, then they are as much in the dark as you are.

Don't try to meet their expectations because they may well not have any.

Perceived Value

Sometimes clients *want* to pay a high fee!   By paying top dollar, they value the project more, or they prove to their boss that the photographer just hired is the best, or it raises their self-esteem to pay a lot.   And if it's a major project, they also feel skeptical if you charge them too little.

The sale of an old scarf best illustrates this.   An antique clothing dealer paid $5 for a beautiful scarf from the 1930's. She priced it at $15 and displayed it in her shop.   It didn't sell.   "It was truly beautiful and shouldn't have sold for less, so I experimented with raising the price—to $65."   It sold the first day.   By inflating the price, she increased the perceived value of the item.   There are times when you will want to do that with your work.

The Hunch Factor

"Gut feeling" should be your final consideration.   Based on what you've learned of the client, their attitude toward you and the value they place on this particular project, what do you *really* think they will pay? Averaging in the hunch factor will help you decide whether to bid a little high or a little low once you've arrived at what you think your final figure should be. You'll become proficient with experience.

Offering Options Increases Your Opportunity

If, after considering this, you still feel that the client's reaction could surprise you, you may want to consider offering them options. Instead of giving the client one fee, why not come up with two or three by establishing a multi-tier approach to the project?

- "Plan A" would provide every reasonable possibility discussed; little thought would be given to cutting corners.

- "Plan B" might be equally exciting but on a smaller scale. It would still provide the client with much of what was asked.

- "Plan C" might tackle the first step in the problem you have identified, with the option of continuing after initial progress is made.

If your business involves delivering a final product as part of your service, then of course, you will want to show them samples of the variations and the varying costs.

Vital to the tier system is allowing the client to feel that *no matter what they select, it will be a class act*. Though you may express a preference for one plan or another, they should feel that all of them interest you and that if they choose to spend less, it will still get your full attention.

Offering the option of "Plan C" (beginning with one step) can also be helpful when you and the client are considering working together long-term. It gives you both the opportunity to try out the relationship. If it turns out that the client is difficult to work with or interferes with your efforts, you will have time to re-evaluate whether you want them as a client and/or what to charge in light of your new knowledge. By the same token, the client has the opportunity to get to know you and appreciate your work.

IV. "PRE-QUALIFYING" YOUR CLIENT

At this point, you need to take a step back from the effort you've invested in selling yourself, and take a good hard look at the client. Is this really the client for you?

Some clients are destined to be difficult, and if you need the work, you'll likely choose to overlook this. However, no client is worth the trouble if they will be unable to pay when the job is complete. If you're familiar with the client company and know that it is financially sound and respected for paying its bills, fine. You're ready to place your bid. However, if you have any doubts, there are steps to take to protect yourself:

- Do you know someone who has worked for this particular company or individual? If so, call and ask if the company or individual paid promptly.

- Consider getting a credit report on the client, particularly if you might have to expend money for them. According to the Associated Credit Bureaus, you should be able to buy a credit report on any business or individual for $15-20. Check the Yellow Pages for credit bureau services. Dun & Bradstreet has a credit service that will fax reports to you. For a one-time check, it's about $60; if you need to run many checks throughout the year, you can bring the cost down by signing a regular agreement with them. You might also check with your accountant. Sometimes he or she can get a credit check done for you for less than you might pay otherwise.

If you would like to work for the client but still have lingering doubts about how quickly they'll respond to your invoice, there are two additional steps you can take:

1. Explain early in the process that you're a small company where cash flow is very important. For that reason, you will need full or partial payment in advance. By making a financial commitment upfront, the client is also demonstrating that they are serious about the task at hand.

2. Refuse to make third-party payments for a client about whom you're concerned. Request that they pay the printer, the furniture company, or the photographer directly. You will be unable to mark up for any effort you've put in to working with the outside vendor, but the downside—being stuck with the bill—is serious enough to make this a worthwhile measure to take.

V. PLACING THE BID

Before we continue, I would like to briefly discuss how your image can affect what happens next. Let's suppose the fee you've settled upon is a high one. If so, an important factor in commanding that fee will be your image. Everything from your attire to your stationery needs to be in line with the look of someone who commands high fees. If your image conveys that you are reliable, tops in your field, and will do a great job, many people will pay for peace of mind to get the job done right.

By the same token, some of you reading this book may be aiming for a different market. You may have done your research and determined that you are better off with a large volume of customers who come to you because of your competitive pricing. If so, while your image should be a

good one, you don't need to set yourself up to be the Rolls
Royce of your industry.

In Person or By Telephone?

Once you're ready to place the bid, should you do it by
telephone or set up an appointment? This depends primarily
upon the size and scope of the job. Negotiations on small
jobs are often handled by telephone; with a large job, you
likely have some sort of presentation to make and so, of
course, presenting your price in person is the thing to do.

Being there is good for negotiation because you have the
opportunity to build enthusiasm for the job through your
presentation. You'll also have the added benefit of being able
to observe the client's reaction. You'll know if he or she is
shocked by the cost; or you may see in his or her face that
your price is low.

When to bring up money? After you've made your presentation and have had the opportunity to intrigue them with what
can be done if they contract for your services.

For small and medium-sized jobs, often the initial in-person
meeting is the only one you'll have, and the client will expect
you to call back with a price. With a telephone call, you're
at a disadvantage because you don't necessarily have the
client's full attention to remind them of the importance of the
job. However, many successful negotiations on smaller jobs
have been completed this way.

If you must submit your price by phone, verify that this is a convenient time to talk about the matter, and offer to call back if you don't feel you have their attention.

Placing the Bid

Be confident. Remind them of exactly what the job is, how much work there is, and what you can do to make their lives easier. The client likely has his or her mind on something else when you first enter the office, and you need to take a few minutes to remind him or her of why you were called in and the problem they were hoping you could solve. Stress:

- How you are going to *help* them. Every client has a "hot button," a nerve you can touch that will remind him or her how very, very important this project is and why it must be done now. Pinpoint exactly what the client wants out of the deal and promise to do that.

- Your ability to do the job. Your professionalism (delivering on time, your resourcefulness, attention to detail, etc.), your enthusiasm for this particular project, and your willingness to go the extra mile for the client.

Unless you've been summoned to do an entire presentation, make your comments succinct and brief, without seeming rushed. Your client may be pressed for time, and you should exhibit that you are in tune with the client's needs and are prepared to make the day easier, not more difficult.

Remember that this is likely to be a negotiation, and if you feel you can (see discussion in Chapter III), set a price a little higher than you need. That way you have some leeway, should they want to negotiate.

When you get to the discussion of money, present your price and wait. Any hesitation or nervousness on your part at this stage is an open invitation for the client to say, "Can you do it for less?"

The Client's Response

Following your announcement, there are generally three possible responses:

- "Yes!" If so, discuss the payment schedule (see Chapter IX), and tell them you'll send them a letter of agreement to be signed and returned to you (see Chapter X). Then get started!

- "We'd like to think it over and get back to you." Try to pin them down to a date (tomorrow? next week? next month?) as to when you might hear from them. Then if you don't hear, you call *them*. Jobs are often lost for lack of follow-up, so be persistent!

If they keep you waiting for very long, consider notifying them that your estimate is only good for a limited period. (After all, your situation may change in that time, making you less interested in tackling the project for the price discussed.) If you have prepared a written proposal, then it is perfectly appropriate to stipulate on the proposal that the price given is good for sixty days. If all your dealings on the project have been verbal, then in a subsequent conversation, you can mention: "I'd love to work with you and will look forward to it, but I should note that my estimate is only good for sixty days. If we were to start the project much beyond that date, my price may be affected." Follow up in writing. A very short business letter expressing continued enthusiasm for the project and the fact that you can only guarantee your price for sixty days is perfectly appropriate.

"Your price is too high." If they've confronted you directly on the price issue then they may be calling your bluff. Don't become defensive, and don't start negotiating yet. Find out what is really behind their remark by meeting them head on: "I'd still like to do the job. What do you recommend?" If they were testing to see if you'd drop your price, they've now learned that you won't without reason. But sometimes a client's knee-jerk reaction on price is actually signalling something else. Maybe they want the work schedule structured differently to put payments in different months. Or sometimes they really want you to do the job, but they want the overall project to come in at a lesser cost. Before you start cutting your own fee, see what's really behind the comment. If they truly feel your fee needs to come down, you have other options, and those will be discussed fully in the next chapter.

"No, we're not interested." Don't drop it here. Consider the following:

a) Can you evaluate by their reaction whether their response was negative because of the fee? If so, you may want to negotiate. (Read the next chapter.) If you're not sure, ask: "Is it my fee?" It's vital that you start getting feedback as to why you do or do not get certain jobs.

b) Did the job go to someone else? Ask why, and inquire about the fee your competitor will receive. Maybe they were less expensive, or maybe they had more experience. Again, it will be helpful to know.

c) If neither of the above occurred, find out what happened. Was there something they needed that you failed to provide? Or did it have anything to do with you? Sometimes projects are shelved (or handled internally) because of a personnel change or an unexpected budget cutback or because the president changed his mind. "However, if the job is simply being tabled for a time, ask when they might re-consider. Again, this gives *you* the opportunity to act by calling back at the appointed time. If there seems little hope of reviving the project, then you'll have to chalk this one up to experience. (And remember, this happens to *everyone* who is self-employed.)

VI. WHAT TO DO WHEN THE CLIENT SAYS "NO"

If this were a fairy tale, then the king would simply turn to the royal advisor and say, "How much are you going to charge me?" and after the royal advisor named his price, the king would say, "Fine, let's have a toast to celebrate." However, we all know that this is no fairy tale, and clients do say, "no."

And no matter how troublesome the client was going to be or how little they understood about the project to be undertaken, once we've gone to the effort of bidding on the job, it's always a big disappointment when the client turns us down. "Okay, I'll do it for less!" is *not* the right response!

Whatever the problem, *maintain your confidence.* If you remain calm and unapologetic, they may decide they are the ones who misjudged the job.

Also consider: *Do you really want to negotiate?* If you've set what you feel is a fair price and they won't meet it, then you may simply prefer to walk away, saying: "That's my price. I'm disappointed you can't meet it." (Besides, if they don't find someone as well-qualified, they might call back.)

One business owner reminded me: "The best reason to lose a job is because you asked too much money." Pride in yourself and pride in being treated as a well-respected professional is vital to your long-range business success.

Cut Back or Redesign

However, there may be reasons why you want to salvage the deal. Perhaps you've been going through a dry spell and really need the cash, or maybe there was something about the project (the experience in a new field? the challenge of the problem?) which really caught your fancy. If so, and if you decide to continue to pursue it, recognize from this moment on that you mustn't regret the time or the lack of adequate pay. You are *choosing* to pursue it, and you had a free choice.

Why is this important? Because for any working relationship to go well, it is essential that both parties feel good about it. If you feel taken advantage of, it will reflect in your attitude and probably in the ultimate job you do. If they feel they didn't get your full attention, it can lead to bad word-of-mouth.

Why not propose that the two of you work out a way to trim the job, break it into affordable sections, or redesign it?

Suppose you have just received the answer that they'd love to work with you but your fee is simply too high. Your response: "Well, tell me what figure did you have in mind? Perhaps there's a way we can tailor my work to fit that budget."

To modify a job, a publicist could approach a smaller number of publications in seeking publicity for a client; an efficiency expert could tackle one segment of the job; a marketing consultant could oversee 75 percent of the program discussed.

Consequently, you can get the job (and probably reduce the time involved), and the client will be pleased because the job can proceed for an affordable price. And even if you end up earning less than you had originally hoped, you've maintained a position of strength; they'll never mutter among themselves, "Oh I know he'll do it for less..."

What's more, once you get started and have the opportunity to prove your worth, it's likely that more work with this client will follow. You've got your foot in the door.

VII. WHEN YOUR CLIENT IS A HOMEOWNER OR INDIVIDUAL

After the first edition of **How to Set Your Fees and Get Them** was published, I occasionally heard from readers who wanted to know more about selling one's services to homeowners and individuals rather than to companies.

In essence, the methods are the same. No matter who your customer, the principles of pricing and negotiation outlined here apply to both individuals and corporations. However, I can refine my advice a bit, and this is what I will set out to do.

Educate the Client

In many cases, homeowners or individuals are not all that experienced at hiring outside help. Whether you are a professional organizer, an exercise instructor, a home contractor, or a financial advisor, there's a good possibility that the individual may never have hired a person such as yourself. What's more, they've likely been filled with stories of their neighbors down the street who got bilked by the contractor who was building their deck, or they know a friend whose "cousin does people's taxes for next to nothing..." In other words, they may have little knowledge about what they are getting into, or the knowledge they have may be inaccurate.

Start by assessing their understanding of the project and take the time required to explain the work at hand to them. They'll be more willing to pay the fee you require if they understand exactly what is involved and why it is of benefit to them. For example, the family putting on an addition may decide to manage the job themselves if the home contractor they are considering doesn't impress upon them the amount of time, money, and aggravation he can save them.

Educate Yourself

The homeowner or individual is seeking help for a very specific reason—maybe not the one they say. It is your job to assess what the potential client's true need is. (This is true with corporate clients as well, but when approaching a business the first task is to decide *whose* needs should be addressed.)

Here are some of the motivating factors:

> **Saving Time.** Many people turn to outsiders for help because they feel harried by all the clutter of life. If a client is hiring you to save time, then

consider how many different ways you can serve them with promises of saving time. One clothing store owner arranges for home delivery for her customers if their purchases have been left for tailoring. Smart move. It guarantees her customer loyalty by saving her customers time. See if some aspect of this applies to your business.

Saving Money. Though an outside consultant costs money, frequently they save a client money, too. To the customer, it may seem like a luxury to be assisted by a decorator, but anyone who has ever had to live with or replace what turned out to be a decorating disaster knows that penny-wise can be pound-foolish. If you sense that financial savings are near and dear to a potential customer's heart, stress the aspect of your business where they'll actually save by using you.

Reassurance. Sometimes clients have a good idea of what they want to do but want someone else to make decisions for them. This type of client may require extra hand-holding.

Status. Perhaps your help is being sought so that the client can "keep up with the Joneses or outdo the Joneses." If they are hiring you for status, you can afford to charge more.

Remember, too, there are all varieties of individuals. (Refer to the "What Costs Extra" section of Chapter III.) Some will want to work along with you, which may be a help or a major hindrance. Individuals are also prone to the "they don't know

what they want until after they see what they don't want"
syndrome. Others may be hiring you because they don't want
to be involved. Be sure to assess personality type before
settling on what you're going to charge them.

Selecting How to Present Your Rate

Of course, the major difference between a corporate staff
member and an individual is that the money being spent by
the individual is really *theirs*. For this reason, the discussion
of cost takes on new interest. Individuals, whether it's a
homeowner, a small business owner, or an individual, generally like to know exactly what they are getting into when
it comes to money.

If per day or per hour is the norm in your profession, you
can make this more palatable to an individual by putting a
cap on the project. Like the corporate client, they will be
happier if you promise them a degree of completion at the
end of that capped period of time. The landscaper might not
be able to do the entire yard for a certain sum, but he or she
can promise to do the front and side yard within the dollar
figure the client stipulates, for example.

Project fees, per person, per piece, and flat rates (if you use
flat rates, remember the benefits of printing up a price list)
offer all the advantages and disadvantages they do for any
client (see Chapter II), however with an individual they
primarily increase your likelihood of making a sale by letting
your customer know exactly what your services will cost.

The Importance of Follow Up

Perhaps no where is persistence more important than when selling to an individual. Unlike a corporate employee, there is likely no other person who is particularly interested in whether or not this person gets a certain job done. A classic example is the wife who wants to redecorate and the spouse who is totally disinterested.

The answer is follow up. A little outside enthusiasm can make a big difference. To do this artfully requires getting estimated times from the individual: "When do you think you might be making a decision?" Follow up then. And again, if necessary. If you maintain your eagerness and enthusiasm for whatever the undertaking, the individual is more likely to remain enthusiastic, too. Remember, however, that sometimes life gets in the way of hiring someone to re-write wills or put together a videotape of family history. If you sense that the individual is temporarily overwhelmed, you might take a step back for a short time.

Or if appropriate, add something to your service so that they can go ahead with the project: If you are hoping to be hired to do a family-history videotape, you might say: "Oh, you needn't go through all your old home movies. We can organize them for you and bring it to you for your approval." Helping them over a psychological hurdle or "time problem" can make a big difference. They have called you in because they have a *need*. Anything you can do to help them fulfill that need can make the difference between sale and no sale.

"They Can't Afford Me..."

You quote your price, but they just can't afford you... If they are truly motivated, and truly want to work with you instead of looking for someone cheaper, there may still be a way to do business together.

Suggest ways that they can help you get the job done. One woman who particularly liked the color "eye" of a particular decorator suggested that she pull all the sample fabrics and floor coverings and let him spend an hour at her home selecting what would work best. She did the legwork, he made the choices and was paid on an hourly basis. This type of arrangement can work well for all involved. The decorator pocketed some hourly fees that wouldn't have been his otherwise, and the homeowner got what she considered first-class taste without having to spend a bundle.

VIII. HOW TO HANDLE EXPENSES

When working as an independent contractor, you can generally pass on certain expenses to the client. However, you will want to clarify ahead of time—and in writing—exactly what expenses the client will pay for. That way there will be no surprises for either party.

However, before starting to document every penny you spend on behalf of the client, you need to develop an "expense philosophy."

Remember that part of the reason your hourly rate is 2.5 times that of a staff person's is because you have operating expenses to absorb. Though in some professions you may be able to pass through most expenses to the client, I think most of us are in situations where charging for every penny spent may take more time than it's worth.

As a matter of fact, one attorney reports that he has found it more efficient not to pass on the cost of performing routine tasks for his clients:

"I find that it's not cost-effective for my staff to spend the time noting down every photocopy they make for a client or every time they lick a stamp. As part of my overhead, I cover all minor expenses including phone, copying, and postage. I bill through to the client only those expenses which are really substantial, like paying $30 or $40 for a legal document we may need."

While you certainly shouldn't have to bear extraordinary expenses, there's something unprofessional about nickeling-and-diming a client to death. And as the attorney points out, record-keeping alone may cost you more time than it's worth. Try to establish an "expense philosophy" that will work for you.

The following list offers guidelines on typical expenses:

Telephone Expenses: If you will be passing on long-distance phone charges to the client, check with your long-distance carrier. For a small fee (approximately $10), most of the carriers can provide you with coding to keep track of your calls. For each of your clients, you select a two-digit code number. When you make a call on their behalf, you punch in their code number. Calls on your next bill will be sorted by code, often on separate sheets which you can use to document your invoice for expenses. If this service is unavailable to you, then you may want to keep note of them on a client time sheet (see Appendix), or you may prefer to keep a log of all calls in a notebook. Note the length of the call and the client for whom it was made. You might find it handy to have a stopwatch by the phone.

Fax Machine Charges: Like telephone usage, most fax machine usage should be considered part of overhead. Only a great volume of material sent long-distance might merit being passed through to the client.

Postage and Messengers: If you will be responsible for major mailings for your clients or will need to make frequent use of messengers, then these expenses can be passed on. Don't bill for a few stamps here and there.

If you use a postage meter, then tracking usage on a chart is probably simplest. That way the person putting through the mail can easily note how much went out on a certain day, and those figures can be tabulated at the end of each month or at the end of a billing period. If you do not have a postage meter, then consider simply buying a roll of stamps for each client. When you've gone through a full roll of 100 you'll know exactly what they owe you.

Photocopying: Pass on these charges only if a large volume of copying is involved. If you calculate a per-copy cost on your own copying machine, the amount is fractions of a cent—not worth billing for.

If you have material copied by an outside vendor, it increases your cost, but billing is simplified. Photocopy or offset shops will provide you with receipts to document your costs. If you're doing it in-house and a great volume of material is involved, then set a per-page rate by checking with other business owners to see what they charge, or charge several cents under what is being charged at your local copy shop. See the postage chart in the Appendix. This type of chart could also be used to keep track of copies.

Course Materials: If you are teaching a class or conducting a workshop, the cost of course materials is often billed to the client. If the client is selling your course to outside students, they will often add a "materials" fee to the amount charged for the course.

Printing and Photography: These are directly billable to the client.

Entertainment: If it is necessary that you entertain (whether it's taking one person to lunch or throwing a cocktail party for 100), this would be paid for by the client. Though a major event will probably have been discussed and sanctioned by the client, make sure the guidelines concerning business lunches are outlined carefully. Just because you take a potential contact to lunch doesn't mean that the deal you're working on will come through. Make sure the client understands that.

Travel: Possible plane trips and other long-distance travel costs should be outlined and discussed with your client in advance.

These are standard expenses generally incurred in the course of doing business. However, every field may have its own additional expenses. A home economist who works as an independent consultant passes through her food preparation expenses. She notes that while the cost of two cups of flour can be broken down easily enough, she has to standardize such charges as very small amounts of expensive spices (e.g., she charges 35 cents per spice if the recipe calls for less than a tablespoon). Each business may have its peculiarities, so think about the costs you are likely to incur and establish a system of your own.

Setting a Limit

You and the client will also want to agree on a way to limit expenses. Typically, the independent contractor agrees to a figure not to be exceeded (per day or per week or per expense category) without the client's okay. These limits should be spelled out in the letter of agreement that is discussed in the next section.

Expenses For Subcontracted Work

Essentially, subcontracting (hiring others to perform certain functions for your client) falls into two different categories:

1) **The Client Doesn't Know.** Perhaps your business concerns evaluating a company implementation of equal opportunity requirements, but you hate writing up the evaluations of each company. Then you might hire a writer to put together the required document. Does the client need to know about the writer? Of course not. If you're an old hand at subcontracting, then you budget in advance for what the writer will cost you and make it up as you see fit—you could charge anywhere from 15-20 percent what you paid right up to four times the writer's fee. (And remember, this is saving you time that the client won't have to pay for at your rates.) What you can charge simply depends on the budget for the overall project. Too high a mark-up on subcontracting may raise your overall fee so high that you don't get the job, so always evaluate whether or not you are pricing yourself out of the market. Of course, neither your proposal nor your bill would make any mention of this expense. This is part of the "overhead" on the project, and one on which you can make a profit.

2) **The Client Knows.** In the fields of advertising and design, it is quite common for the entrepreneur to do what amounts to advancing money to the client company. If a typesetter, a photographer, and a printer will be needed to complete a particular

project, then a designer or art director would get initial estimates from them to include as part of his own estimate. However, in most cases, the entrepreneur's quote would be a total sum. He would not break out the separate costs. For the entrepreneur's trouble and his role as the contractor, there is generally a standard mark-up of between 15-17.65 percent. Unless the company has specifically asked for the bills and instructed you as to what mark-up you can take, your bill would simply reflect the overall cost of the project.

Taking Extra Precautions

If you have any concern about a client's ability to pay (see Chapter IV), think carefully when it comes to major expenses. Other arrangements can and should be made under certain circumstances. The graphic artist who would normally pay the printer for a brochure (and mark it up slightly before billing the client) would be wise to arrange for an under-capitalized new business to pay the printer directly. No potential mark-up is worth the possibility of being stuck for your client's bill.

When it comes to a major expense such as air travel, consider asking for the client to arrange for (and pay for) your ticket through their corporate travel department or agency. This would be appropriate with a client who stretches out payments, thereby delaying your reimbursement. It's also good thinking for consultants working as expert witnesses in court cases. This kind of work makes you subject to many variables (do you arrive only to find the case is postponed? does your client suddenly decide you are unnecessary, etc?), and you certainly don't want your expense check caught up in a dispute. By asking the client to make arrangements, it lessens your chance of trouble.

Clarifying expenses verbally and in writing will prevent major problems. Careful record-keeping will also be essential. Retain all receipts and note your expenses carefully. You should always be able to substantiate what you spend.

IX. SCHEDULE OF PAYMENT

In addition to resolving how much you're going to be paid, it is also vital that you clarify with the client *when* you will be paid.

In most cases, you will want to ask for some money in advance. For the most part, self-employed professionals are providing a specialized service for the client. There is no product involved. If payment is not forthcoming, there is no way to step in and take back what you've given them. If someone fails to pay for their refrigerator or living room couch, you can bet that the item will be re-claimed. But even if you were to take back a report, a design, or an evaluation, they may still use some of the ideas, and there is little you can do about it.

By collecting part of the payment at the outset, you accomplish several things:

- You have established that this is a legitimate client, who, in the beginning anyway, intends to pay your bill.

- You have guaranteed that you will receive at least part of the payment for your services. (They could stiff you later on, but so far so good.)

- You have run a small but important test on an unknown client—they have given you a valid check.

Upon receipt of this first payment, photocopy the check or note the name of the bank and the address. Should the client fail to make good on other payments and you need to take him or her to court, knowing the name of the client's bank can help.

Don't expect checks to arrive by magic. Send invoices for advance payments, for installment payments, for expense billings, for retainer agreements... If they owe you money, you should send them a bill for it.

To establish a schedule of payments on a project, consider the following:

Short-term Projects

Ask for one-third to one-half of the payment at the start of the project with the balance due within 10-30 days of completion. They're asking you to work in good faith. Why shouldn't they pay in good faith?

Long-term Projects

Set up a series of dates when the payments are due. If the overall fee is $3000 over a period of six months, then you may want to be paid in six equal installments. Specify the date of the month (i.e., the first or the tenth) when each $500 payment would be due. Or you may prefer for the fee to be paid in three installments of $1000 each, perhaps one payment made in advance, and each of the other two made at the completion of some stage of the project. There is no "norm" for this, you simply need to stipulate what you want and negotiate that with the client.

Retainer Agreements

Typically, retainer agreements would provide for monthly payments of specific amounts. You will also want to agree on how additional services above and beyond what the retainer fee covers will be paid, how they will be billed, and when due.

Reimbursement for Expenses

When will you bill for expenses, and when can you expect that bill to be paid? In long-term relationships, it will probably be most convenient to submit your bill for expenses prior to an upcoming payment so that payment will be added to your next check. Discuss with the client the best schedule for accomplishing this.

Where To Bill

In addition to discussing the schedule of payments, ask your client these questions:

- Where should the bill be sent? To the client directly or to the accounting department?

- What special information (purchase order number, project name, department, etc.) should be included in order to speed the processing of the invoice?

X. THE LETTER OF AGREEMENT

No matter how well you like or trust the person with whom you're going to work, always put your agreement in writing. It is an opportunity for both parties to see that they have reached a mutual understanding about the work to be done. Furthermore, should anything go wrong, you are protected.

In most cases, a simple business letter which provides for the signature of both parties will constitute a perfectly acceptable agreement. It is also preferable to originate the letter because you can write it with your own interests in mind.

Writing Your Own Letter

When creating your own letter, "legal-ese" is not necessary. Simply write exactly what you mean in clear English. A standard letter of agreement would contain the following:

- **What will you provide?** Be specific enough that you define your duties (so that they can't expect more from you), but take care of yourself. For example, don't volunteer any extras or any results you can't guarantee.

- **When is the project due, or how long is the relationship to last?** Specify the agreed-upon time frame.

- **What will the client provide?** Are they to give you access to personnel? Research materials? Word-processing services? Also specify *when* these services are to be provided, i.e., "Research materials are to be delivered by May 10." Completion of your responsibilities may hinge on the client delivering information to you, so you need to specify in your letter that they have deadlines to meet, too.

- **Are there any special terms which need to be specified?** For example, perhaps there was uncertainty as to how quickly the client could provide you with research material, and therefore, special arrangements were made and agreed to regarding the project due date: "As we discussed, if the research material is provided on schedule (by December 15), then the project will be completed by January 15. If the research material is delayed by the possible week to ten days discussed, then the project due date will be extended to January 25."

- **What is the fee and when is it to be paid?** Spell out the complete timetable. Also provide for a rate of pay for additional services provided. For example, your project fee might be $5000, but at what rate will you charge if additional work above and beyond what was agreed upon is required?

- **How can the agreement be terminated?** Always specify how either party may bring the agreement to an end. Method of notification (phone, certified letter, etc.) and the required time period for notification should be specified (termination on receipt of phone call or letter? at the end of the next billing period?) These provisions will depend on the nature of your work and the circumstances under which either party might want to terminate.

- **How can a dispute be resolved?** Small Claims Court and arbitration are the two most useful ways to resolve any dispute (see Chapter XI). In your letter of agreement, you may want to provide for this: "Any disputes in excess of (maximum limit of your local small claims court, often $5,000) arising out of our agreement shall be submitted to binding arbitration before a mutually agreed upon arbitrator." Should this step become necessary, check with the American Arbitration Association for more information.

Many professional organizations have sample letters of agreement available that would cover the points that need to be clarified in the interests of their membership. Contact them and inquire. You may gain some additional pointers.

Put the letter on your own letterhead stationery, and use a business format so that the client's full name and address appear as well. At the bottom of the last page, type "Agreed to by_____" with a space for the personal signature and the name of their company. If the letter runs more than one page, both parties should initial any pages which do not include their signature. (See the Appendix for sample letters of agreement.)

Getting it Returned

What if they don't sign the letter and return it? Most business owners insist that the letter be signed and returned before work will begin. One entrepreneur stipulates at the bottom of her agreements: "No assignment will be started until a signed agreement and the required advance payment have been received." You could also simply phone to remind them why their project is not yet underway.

When to Consult an Attorney

Though in most cases, your own letters of agreement will be perfectly serviceable, there will be times when you will need to consult a lawyer:

1) If the business agreement is complex or if the client is a formidable force, get legal help.

2) If you are dealing with a major company which has its own contract for non-staff professionals to sign, ask an attorney to read it over for you. Then don't be afraid to request modifications to the agreement. It will likely be a standard agreement, so there may be conditions to which you needn't agree or terms which you might wish to add.

3) If you provide similar services to many clients, a
   standard contract or agreement will be helpful.
   Literary agents who provide similar services to
   writers they represent or consultants who do many
   workshops are just two examples where a standard
   contract written by a lawyer might be helpful.

To keep your legal expenses in check, provide detailed
information to your attorney by compiling answers to the
questions given above. You may even want to write the
agreement yourself and simply ask the attorney to look it
over.

The time and/or money you spend in developing a sound letter
of agreement will be well worth it. At some point in the
future, you'll be glad you protected yourself.

Also remember, if the client doesn't live up to his part of the
bargain, you can take him to Small Claims Court. At very
little expense, many business owners have seen their rights
upheld there.

XI. COLLECTION

Part of being in business for yourself is having to be chairman and bill collector, too. You may have just lunched at the finest restaurant in town, but at 2:30 p.m. you'll need to go back to the office to look over the outstanding accounts.

In your letter of agreement, you have stipulated when you are to be paid. Despite the fact that both parties know that money is due at a certain time, provide the client with an official invoice. You can buy invoices from an office supply store or design one on your computer. (If you use a simple design on letterhead, be certain to number each invoice to make it easier to keep track of payments and amounts still due on various bills.)

Send your invoice directly to the appropriate person or department. Remember that the invoice may or may not go directly to the client—sometimes they want you to send it to a specific person in the accounting department. Be sure to learn the system and follow it. It will often speed things up. Bill promptly, and don't include anything else in the envelope. It may distract the recipient.

Invoices should either be submitted at the time of delivery of the work or on the date(s) stipulated in the letter of agreement, and common practice is that bills are due within thirty days. Establish a system to monitor this. (Some computer programs will keep track of this data, or you can date-file a copy of the bill. Or consider making a calendar notation that Client X should have paid by a certain date.)

Remind promptly--and by phone. On the 31st day after you sent your invoice, call. Written communication isn't nearly as effective as telephone contact. In the course of your phone call, you need to find out exactly when they plan to send the check, and verify the amount they are sending. Follow this phone call with another copy of the bill. Should you ever need to take the client to court for non-payment you will want evidence to demonstrate that your efforts to collect were repeatedly ignored.

If the bill is still unpaid on the new date specified, then the time has come for a more serious approach. Contact the client (even if up until now you've been in touch with someone in accounting), and find out what the problem is.

Ways to Encourage Prompt Payment

Here are some tried-and-true tactics that can help you get paid on time:

- Some business owners have great success offering a 2-5 percent discount on bills paid within ten days. You might experiment with this to see if it helps in your business. Print the offer on the lower portion of each invoice. The prompt-paying client will benefit, and you'll be saved time in working on collection.

- Check your state's usury laws to find out how large a percentage can be charged on overdue bills. At the bottom of the bill you may want to stipulate that a charge of "x" percent (usually 1-1.5 percent per month) will be added for each month the bill is overdue. Some business owners send a note after twenty days, reminding the client that they'll owe a "late" charge if they don't pay within the next ten days.

- In your business can you accept credit cards? This gives you the money due you and lets the credit card company shoulder any collection headaches.

- Get as much money upfront as you can.

- Stop servicing the account if your bill remains unpaid.

When They Can't Pay

Be patient. Suggest a new payment schedule that they might be able to meet. (At this point, slow pay is better than no pay.) And remember, *persistence is key.* Just as follow-up can make all the difference in whether you get a job, follow-up will help you get paid. "The squeaky wheel gets the grease," may first have been said by a bill collector.

If ever you feel frustrated, keep in mind this story about a counselor I know. On retainer with a private school that was having financial difficulty, she was consistently paid. How?

"I realized that in order to be paid, I'd need to make myself known," she said. "So I simply make it part of my routine to show up in the accounting office on the first of every month. I sit and wait until they draw my check, and they haven't missed a payment yet!"

In general, it is wisest to try to motivate the client to want to pay. The longer you can keep the relationship from being adversarial, then the better off you are. However, if there is still a problem after two and a half months, then you may need a letter or phone call from your attorney, or consider a collection agency. Most require no money in advance and take a percentage of what they collect; sometimes almost 1/3 of small amounts, usually taking a smaller percentage as the amount collected rises above $3,000 or $4,000.

Your Client is Going Bankrupt?

What happens if the company for whom you're working runs into financial difficulty? If the problem is a bad check, call and say: "I know you intend to make good on this, but how do you suggest we work this out?" Otherwise, your best bet is to try to be among those who are first in the door for payment. A letter from your attorney may help get you an earlier payment. If all else fails, be willing to bargain. Offer to settle for equipment, furniture, or supplies instead of cash. It will be easier than suing a company that is going belly up.

If they declare bankruptcy before you are paid, you will need to file a claim against the company. (You should be sent a form automatically, but call to be certain that you will be.) You can also contact the appropriate bankruptcy court. Get the number of the case file and ask for a claim form. The good news? Your cost of filing is only the cost of a postage stamp. The bad news? Payment for a company in bankruptcy is generally ten cents on the dollar.

Small Claims Court

This is an inexpensive way to solve minor collection problems—generally good for claims of about $1000 (always less than $5,000). The downside to small claims court is that you generally need to file in the jurisdiction of the company that owes you money which may be problematic if it isn't local. Also, though you may get a judgment against the client, you will still need to arrange to collect the money. However, there are definite benefits to using small claims court:

- You don't need a lawyer.

- There is usually a quick resolution. Generally the hearing is only a few weeks after a complaint is filed.

- It gives you an opportunity to communicate with a client who may have been stonewalling you.

Check in the local phone directory under Government Offices. If there is no listing for "small claims court," call the county clerk for advice. If you're unsure of the county in which your client is based, check with the county clerk to make sure you have the right court. Be sure you have the proper legal name for the company you're suing.

When you arrive at the court, you will need to fill out a complaint form—the cost of which is generally $2-10. On the form you'll be providing yours and the defendant's name and address and a brief description of why you're suing and the damages claimed.

While there, you should get a hearing date--usually in about two weeks—and the defendant will be notified by mail.

To prepare for the hearing (which will last only 10-15 minutes), gather evidence—your contract, a report on work performed for the client, anything that explains your side of the story. You will also need to prove that you have tried other collection methods before coming to court, so save documents or evidence of the effort you made. Notations about follow-up phone calls may help.

Arrive on time. Generally the court will encourage you and the defendant to settle it beforehand, with a clerk on hand to explain any legal technicalities. If the judge is backed up, you may be offered an arbitrator instead. This can be perfectly satisfactory, but keep in mind that the arbitrator's opinion is final.

A study shows that your chances at winning are good. Even if the defendant shows up, he has only a 25 percent chance of winning. It's not all good news: you may not get all you're asking, and you may have trouble collecting.

If the defendant fails to appear, you will be able to tell your side of the story to an arbitrator who will generally award you the appropriate damages, generally including court costs. If the defendant fails to pay after this judgment, call and ask how to use law-enforcement personnel to collect your judgment. In some cases, a lien can be placed against the client's property, or if you know where the client banks, a court officer can go to the bank with a writ of execution to obtain your money.

In the long run, an ounce of prevention is worth a pound of cure. Pre-qualify your clients (choose to work for clients with reputations for paying their bills), get a good chunk of your money upfront, and then bill promptly. If at any time payment is late, act immediately: Follow up, pause in your work for them if necessary, or work out an amended payment schedule—that way you needn't lose a client, and you needn't take him or her to court either.

XII. HOW TO AVOID POTENTIAL PITFALLS

No matter how carefully we plan, there are always situations that raise questions. Here are a few that cause concern.

The Advisability of Donating One's Services

Especially when we're starting out, there is usually the temptation to donate one's services, with the hope of being hired for another job later. This can be a great way to get your business started. If you've never had direct experience in a particular area but know you could do it, it provides you with an opportunity to prove your worth.

However, once you've been established for a time, you'll want to carefully consider any situation when you'll be working without pay. If it's to work as a volunteer for your professional organization or to donate services to a worthy cause, that's great. We should do more of that. However, if someone tries to convince you that speaking before a certain group at no charge will be great exposure for you, take a minute to study the situation realistically. Who is the audience? What publicity will you get from it? Will you be able to sell your services to this group? Will you really gain exposure to more than just a handful of people?

It's easy to feel flattered and want to oblige when someone indicates that they "just can't plan the program without you," but I've found—as have many of my colleagues—that sometimes the return really isn't worth the time. If you'll get good publicity, or if the audience consist of people who could hire you, or if you want to do a favor for the person who asked you, then do it! Otherwise, don't think twice about saying, "no."

What To Do When the Job Turns Sour

Every now and then things don't go as planned. Perhaps the client forgets he only retained you for three months of services and keeps calling to "ask a few questions," or perhaps you get into a project and realize you've badly underestimated the work involved.

What you do, of course, depends on the exact circumstances, but remember that you are a professional, and you needn't be taken advantage of. For example, the client who keeps calling for additional advice should be politely reminded, on the second or third call, that you really can't dispense free information, and if they would like to pay you for this consultation then you'd be happy to continue the conversation.

If you've misjudged a job (or they misrepresented it) and feel you can't afford to continue with it, you need to refer to your letter of agreement to see what your termination options are. Then evaluate what is at stake. If this is a client with whom you'd like to maintain a relationship, then you may decide you have to keep at it but at the same time you need to find an opportunity to mention that you under-estimated the job. Though you shouldn't expect additional payment, you need to clue them in on your error so that the next time you price a job for them, they'll understand why it will cost more than your previous project did.

Shouldn't you simply admit your mistake and ask for more money? Most entrepreneurs find this is a sure-fire way to lose a client. Though the client may be understanding and agreeable at the time, the relationship is rarely the same afterwards.

But perhaps you're in over your head and you'd just like to quit. Then you may want to cut your losses by stopping and delivering what you've done thus far. Discuss the problem with them to see if you can agree on a settlement. While you may not be paid in full for your efforts, at least you've extricated yourself from a poor situation and the possibility of a greater loss of time and money.

Delivering What Was Ordered

Sometimes the self-employed get so caught up in the process of what they are doing that they forget they must operate as a business.

When you were on staff, some projects probably went beautifully and were really something to be proud of while others were assignments to forget. Being in business for yourself is no different. Of course, we all strive to produce more of the projects we're proud of, but inevitably, sometimes we're little more than a hired hand.

If you get caught up in perfecting absolutely everything you do, it will be difficult to come out ahead and stay in business for yourself. While in no way am I advocating sloppy workmanship or inattention to detail, I do think you should acknowledge that if someone is only paying for Plan C of the options you gave him, then don't try to deliver Plan A anyway.

Big Job vs. Small Job

Unfortunately, six small jobs requiring ten hours each do not equal one big job requiring sixty hours. *It takes time to shift gears.*

If you've been in business for a time, then you may be wondering how to tactfully discourage the clients who need only an hour or two of your time now and then—the very same clients who may have helped to get you started. One logical method is to establish that you will only take jobs that meet a certain time or dollar minimum. That way if the client really wants to hire you they know what the terms are, and yet you aren't stuck selling an hour here or an hour there.

But one word of warning before you trade in your smaller clients: Don't ever sell your soul to one giant. An entrepreneur must always keep an eye out for the possibility that a major client may drop by the wayside. What if the business for whom you're consulting is sold? What if the person with whom you work is fired? What if the company goes bankrupt? If you've tied your business to their coattails, you may be in for a rude awakening. The smart business person will take on a major client but will always balance it with other clients in order to protect against disaster.

XIII. FEE-SETTING Q & A

Through speaking engagements and teaching a course on fee-setting, I hear a good number of questions on the topic. Here are some interesting ones.

- **What do you do in a "test" situation? What do you say when the client asks you to create a sample of your work specifically for them before they decide whether or not to hire you?**

Basically, this is working on speculation, and most of the time, you would be wise to show similar samples of your work and answer: "I'm sorry, I can't afford to work that way. You've seen samples of my previous work, and if you'd like to go ahead with a firm commitment, I'm available. Otherwise, I'll have to pass." Most business owners have fallen for one of these try-outs at some time or another only to regret it—the project is shelved, someone else gets the job (and as the facts become known it is obvious the other person would have gotten it anyway), or worse—the business owner later sees his or her ideas implemented by someone in-house!

However, there may be times when you will want to be considered for a particular job despite having to create a sample. Advertising agencies, architects, and designers are among those who are often placed in a situation where they are one of three or so companies asked to prepare a presentation to compete for a particular account. If the stakes are high and this is the industry norm, you don't want to pass it up. (You can usually bill for your out-of-pocket expenses for this type of presentation.)

Before going ahead, determine the size of the account which awaits you if you do get the job. Unless you are just starting out, this type of speculative effort is generally only worthwhile if the rewards are great.

You'll also want to develop a sense of when the presentations are being done for competitive reasons (meaning that the company with the best price and best presentation will get the job) or when it is simply comparative (meaning that the vice president really wants to use the agency or person he's used before, but he's required to see other presentations and get comparative bids). You don't want to waste your time helping someone else get the job.

- **How do you feel about offering free consultations? Do you think they diminish one's value?**

The answer to this partly depends on the situation, but there are many times that a "free consultation" is really just a different way of making a sales call. Suppose a public relations person approaches you and wants to come in and show you her work (sales call)—would you set up an appointment? Most of us wouldn't. But if she calls and offers a "free consultation" to discuss a public relations strategy for your company, would you see her? It can be a good way to get a foot in the door.

Of course, when you're the one offering the free consultation, the trick lies in making the sale. You need to avoid those people who won't hire you no matter how great you are. With those whom you feel might hire you, you need to tantalize without giving away more than you need to. The professional organizer can stress the benefits of organization and offer general advice while stressing to the client that it would be easy for a professional to implement the new system quickly; the direct mail consultant can comment on how effective a direct mail campaign could be (complete with industry statistics) and discuss in general terms how he or she foresees running a campaign unique to that business, etc.

- **How does one bill for the time spent investigating and drawing up proposals for potential clients? Is there a way to monetarily compensate for the amount of hours spent developing new business pitches?**

In general, you will not be able to earn money for the time spent looking for new business. This is the marketing time that we discussed earlier, and it's part of the reason you're billing out your hours at several times what you would be making on staff.

Occasionally, however, there are opportunities to bill for this time. In situations where a great deal has gone into the preparation of a proposal, you may want to inflate your fee to cover yourself for this time. And *if* you get the job, then you will receive compensation. After all, the proposal is almost certainly the first step in any work you will do for them, so it is billable time.

In the advertising industry where elaborate proposals are the norm, many new-business proposals are done on speculation, but increasingly, agencies are beginning to request "development fees." When trying to woo a major advertiser, it is not uncommon for thousands of dollars to be spent in out-of-pocket expenses. Generally, the fee requested would cover expenses, not time, but at least it helps compensate for the effort and cost of being considered for the job.

- **Any special advice for people serving as expert witnesses in court cases?**

To begin, you need to set an appropriate rate for your services. Many of the guidelines already outlined in the book will apply, but keep in mind that you certainly want to charge at least as much as you would charge if you were spending the day at work. If your medical practice brings in $200 an hour, then that's the minimum rate for which you should testify. Also consider whether you are unique. Are you the only person qualified to testify? If so, you can probably charge more. (In some cases, your fees will be subject to review by the judge, and this may affect what you can afford to charge.)

This brings us to point number two: *Who* is going to pay your bill? The defense attorney? The prosecution? The insurance company? The defendant? The defendant's family? Does it come out of court funds? Find out who the true client is before going too far with the discussion. This is also the time to evaluate whether or not you're comfortable with which "side" you're on.

Your client may request a lower fee for your waiting time— the time spent waiting to give your testimony. If you can remain in your office but available by phone, you can lower your waiting fee; otherwise, you will likely need to charge the same hourly rate you charge for testifying.

Expenses such as air travel or overnight accommodations should be paid by the client. Your fee should also be collected in advance; collection post-verdict can be difficult if not impossible. Some attorneys hand their witnesses the check in the courtroom and bring out in testimony that the witness has already been paid. This is to indicate to the jury that the fee is not dependent upon giving a specific "favorable" testimony.

The work can be a good and interesting way to increase income, but before you get involved, be sure you've covered all of the above.

- **After working for less than an hour, I hit upon a perfect solution for my client. Once implemented, the idea will have a wide-ranging effect on the company. Billing them for only an hour seems ludicrous; what do I do?**

Every now and then a consultant will hit upon the perfect idea for a company in only a few minutes. So do you bill them for $75 and let it go at that? Absolutely not.

There's a wonderful story about a town in Colorado that lost its power and couldn't get it back on again. Someone remembered there was an old engineer still living who had helped install the original power system. They tracked him down and asked him to come take a look at it. He went into the plant, took out a little mallet, and walked through to a switch where he went tap, tap, tap. All the power came back on. He spent the town a bill for $5000.02 and itemized it:

"Tapping   2 cents

Knowing where to tap $5000.00"

Sometimes *you* have to bill for "knowing where to tap." And there's a good reason why.

Let's suppose you went into Tiffany's to buy a really lovely diamond ring. On your second visit the salesperson says, "I've been thinking a lot about it, and I've found the perfect ring for you. I polished it up last night, and I just know you're going to love it. The best part is that it's only $20.00!" Wouldn't you be suspicious? Well, your client is going to be equally suspicious if you try to convince him or her that you only need $20 to cover the time it took you to think up the idea that is going to boost their productivity or improve their advertising results, or provide them with a more workable personnel system, etc.

In this type of situation, you need to bill for perceived value (see Chapter III). The client needs to pay for worth of the project—not the few minutes it took you to develop the idea but the years you have spent in the business and the time you have spent solving similar problems for other clients. Almost assuredly, a novice couldn't have thought of the idea as quickly as you did (if they could come up with it at all). All the questions we've asked earlier (who ordered that the project be undertaken?, what is the budget for it?, how will the program be used?, etc.) come into play.

One consultant estimated that it took her about six minutes to come up with a specific solution to a company's problem. Ultimately she charged them $6,000 for her plan. While every job won't work out that well, I wish for you one like that every few years!

- **What are some of the changes that are occurring in fee-setting?**

One trend is the increasing use of the contingency fee which is fully discussed in Chapter II.

Otherwise, there are several industries where changes are taking place. Executive recruiters used to charge a standard 1/3 of the first year of an executive's cash compensation. Now clients are asking for concessions. In return for lowering their percentage slightly (down to 28-30 percent of compensation) for major clients, some executive recruiters are requesting contracts for longer retainers. They are giving up higher income for greater security. Other search firms are asking for a larger proportion of the fee upfront as a way to compensate. Still others are accepting fixed-fee assignments.

The advertising industry is also undergoing change. Previously, many agencies charged a 15 percent commission on the money a client spent on space or time advertising. Clients felt this led to the purchase of more ads, not necessarily better advertising. Slowly, agencies are beginning to use incentive-based fee systems where part of their fee is calculated based on the success of the product they are advertising. Sometimes this is combined with a slightly lower commission. One major agency lowered its's base commission to 13 percent of media billings and will gradually increase it back up to a 15 percent ceiling, contingent upon sales or market share. On the incentive plan, some agencies are asking for a larger piece of business (overseeing more of the communication program) in order to have more control over the success of the product.

Over the next few years, I think there will even be some changes in the way attorneys handle billings. Law firms have long pressured junior lawyers to keep their client-hours up in order to bill time directly to the client. And though there has been a great deal of talk about how the system rewards inefficiency (long hours) instead of fast and efficient workmanship, few companies have changed their habits. However, some experimentation is beginning to take place. In a survey conducted by Price Waterhouse, there is some interest in beginning to experiment with new ways such as discounting, fixed or capped fees, contingency payments, and fee estimates. Clients who formerly asked no questions are beginning to ask about legal budgets, and they want to discuss them. There has been auditing of the billings, and it is becoming apparent that what clients value is efficiency, on-time delivery, predictability of expenses, and pricing that is competitive. However, one aspect of the legal field will never change: Clients will always pay top dollar to the attorney whom they feel can help them win a case.

XIV. WHEN TO RAISE YOUR PRICES AND HOW TO DO IT WITHOUT LOSING CUSTOMERS

There are several important times when you may want to consider raising your fees:

1) **When you feel the market will bear it**. If you're running into situations where the client doesn't even blink at what you are charging, then there is probably good reason to think about re-investigating the current going rate. You may be charging too little.

2) **When you don't really want a job**. Sometimes something will come across your desk which looks like it will take a lot of time and be difficult to do well. Rather than walk away from it, you may

want to consider setting a higher price. One business owner who had been working for $100 per day got tired of the service he was providing and wanted to change businesses. Since he still continued to get calls for his original service, he kept raising his price and was soon commanding $280 daily for the work he had been doing for $100!

3) **When your business has expanded to the point that you can't handle much more work.** If you're that busy, then it's a good opportunity to raise your fees. You may want the rate increases to affect new clients only, or you may decide to notify all clients that as of a certain date your rates are going up. Those who value your services will stay with you.

4) **Annual increases.** Some business owners use annual increases as a way to raise their prices slowly, rather than having a larger increase every few years. However, annual increases are really only necessary if your own business expenses are going up substantially. A negative aspect of raising your fee is that you run the risk of losing clients. If you've researched the going rate and are working for a price you feel is fair then there's no reason to increase your rate just for the sake of doing so.

If you plan on annual increases, present this information to clients in a matter-of-fact way. If you have a contract that extends for more than a year, you'll want to include wording that covers your annual increase. Warning the client will make it easier to establish the new fee when the time comes.

The Importance of an Annual Review

While annual increases every year aren't necessarily important, annual reviews are. Go over the time various jobs took and what your fee was for each. Were you accurate in estimating your price? If not, where did you slip up, and how can you improve for the next year?

Now look at your overall income and expenses. Did your fees cover expenses and leave some left over for profit? If not, can you afford to increase your fee (will the market bear an increase?), or do you need to trim expenses?

Finally, listen to the industry tom-toms. Take a day, or a lunchtime or two, to gossip. Call the people in your business whom you know "always know everybody's business," and find out if rates have been going up recently. If your competition is raising their rates, you may decide to promote the fact that you offer the best price, or you may decide you're ready for an increase, too.

Taking stock at the end of each year provides you with the opportunity to fine-tune your fee-setting system so that it will continue to serve you well in the years to come.

How to Raise Rates

Raising rates on new clients mainly takes confidence. You may find it easier to write down your new rate structure and keep it at hand until you feel totally comfortable with the new figures. If ever confronted with having done an assignment for someone else for less, simply remind them that costs have gone up over time, and develop a sales line to remind them you're good: "I'm very fast and I've worked in this area before. I'm sure you'll be pleased with the results."

Raising rates on old clients is more difficult. Some clients are so valuable that you may not want to tamper with the fee structure right now. Perhaps they send you referrals (in which case you'll want to be sure to tell them you're raising your rates for others), or they may be easy to work with, easy to please, and thankfully, pay regularly and on time. If so, you may want to continue working with them at the rate set previously. (Obviously, you will want to increase their rate at some point to avoid feeling resentful of the work.)

Other current clients will be less valuable. They may be difficult to work for, or perhaps you work for them only occasionally. If you bill by the project, then simply start inflating the quotes you give them on various jobs. If you bill by the day, the head, or per piece, or on retainer, then notify them in writing. Send a personal letter explaining that as of a certain date your fees will go up, that you will continue to be attentive to their needs and will look forward to serving them in the future. No explanation of the price increase is needed, but if you prefer, you can attribute it to "rising costs," or whatever. If the price increase does drive them away, you always knew that was a possibility.

Other Ways to Increase Your Income

- Increase your prices by 10 percent and then offer a 10 percent discount to those whom you don't want to lose.

It establishes a higher rate for your service while still letting your old and valued customers pay the same price.

- Re-describe your service. Stress different aspects of your basic service, and increase the price for it.

- Break your basic service into multiple services, and charge so that the new sum total is higher than your old package price. You may even gain a few new clients who are attracted by being able to hire you for a smaller portion of your service.

- Offer a "Gold Star" version of your service. If you add in something extra (next day delivery, added service that saves the client time or footwork, etc.) you can charge more.

- Customize your service. Can your service be personalized or even more specifically tailored to the client? Offer this at a premium price.

- Raise your prices during premium months and offer a discount during slower ones. A moving company might have one rate for the summer when more families move, and then offer a discount to try to increase business in the winter.

- Use fee escalators to reward success. If you're performing a service where successful results can be measured, provide in your letter of agreement that you will receive a higher fee if certain goals are reached or that you'll be paid a percentage on sales above an agreed-upon base. You can apply this to reward yourself for a superb (and already well-paying) job well done, or you can use it to make a lower-paying job work out for you.

- Offer extra services. Add the option of a follow-up training session following the implementation of a new program you've recommended, for example. The client pays one price for basic services; a higher price if they want the follow-up.

- Add other people's products or services to your line and charge more. A professional organizer might provide a helpful book on getting organized as part of the higher-priced package.

- Does your business lend itself to offering a safe guarantee? If so, offer one and charge more for it.

- For a speech or a performance, ask for a percentage of the amount the organization makes.

All these methods offer you the opportunity to increase your income without scaring off your original customer base. Give one or all of them a try!

XV. BILLING FOR STAFF MEMBERS

Pricing one's services is a continuing challenge for businesses of all sizes.

My original feeling when writing this book was that it was primarily needed by self-employed entrepreneurs who probably work alone or with a single partner. While this is most definitely the case, as I write the subsequent editions, I can also report that among my customers are many firms which range from employing two or three staff members to having hundreds, and their billings vary from a few thousand dollars to million-dollar accounts! You see, even major companies wonder about their fee-setting methods!

Of course, the main difference when it comes to billing is not the size of the company but the fact that the larger business must take into account its staff.

For this reason, we now need to examine how to bill for staff members. The assumption here is that you are figuring your rate on some sort of time basis (where the amount of time worked determines the fee charged). While we have discussed several other types of billing systems, most businesses still need to know how well they are compensated per hour or per day, so the following discussion will focus on a time billing method.

How To Factor Staff Costs Into Your Price

If you have a partner and/or employees, everyone in the company should have an hourly rate for billing. The junior attorney, the paralegal, the senior draftsman--all must have a starting point from which to bill. General clerical help is usually considered part of overhead, however, if you sometimes use a secretary for conducting a specific research project, then her role would shift to one where she is providing a direct service to the client. In this case, you could comfortably bill out for her time. A full explanation on computing the hourly billing figure is contained in Chapter I, however, in brief—and in the case of staff—it involves taking the hourly rate you pay for a staff person and multiplying that figure by 2.5 (or event 2.8 or 3) to come up with an hourly billing figure. For example, let's suppose that the weekly salary you pay a staff person breaks down to be $5 per hour. Multiply that by 2.5, and his or her billing rate would be $12.50. (As explained earlier, the reason for this multiple figure is to cover overhead such as operating expenses, vacations, and benefits as well as profit.)

What do you do with this figure? Do you tell the client that any time your staff person spends on his or her account it will cost $12.50 an hour? No, and for all the reasons we've discussed. Try billing with a project rate. This involves estimating the number of hours you anticipate each staff person will work and figuring that into your total project estimate.

Let's take a small project as an example. If you have determined that you and your partner each bill time at $30 an hour, and together you anticipate spending ten hours on a project, then the fee thus far is $300 ($30 times 10). Then suppose you estimate you will need about five hours of your staff person's time which is billable (as in the example above) at $12.50 an hour, making his or her efforts worth $62.50 (5 times $12.50). Of course, before placing a final bid at that price, you would first test the figure by going through the steps outlined in Chapter III.

In another case, two or three staff people may do the majority of the work on a project, requiring only a few supervisory hours of your time. Again, you estimate the number of hours spent by each person and multiply it by their hourly rate. The result is a total package price. While each project will involve varying combination of hours worked by different people, the formula is always the same.

As suggested previously, you'll find it enormously helpful if you and your staff get in the habit of recording how long you spend on different projects. A design firm may have an artist who does beautiful work but is very slow. There's no reason for this to be a billing problem as long as the firm realizes it must estimate more hours for him or her to do the work than it would for another artist. Many clients are more than happy to pay premium prices for specialized work!

All the basic principles of fee-setting, estimating, and billing apply to all types of businesses, regardless of size. Once armed with these fundamentals, you can use them to get the right rates for you and your staff's services.

XVI. IN THE FINAL ANALYSIS

Every now and then someone will approach me after one of my lectures on fee-setting, describe their dilemma, and then persistently ask and re-ask: "But what would *you* charge?" My answer, of course, is immaterial.

Fee-setting is a process for which there is no right or wrong answer. And if I haven't looked at the project materials, met the people, and done all the work I describe in this book, I have no business offering advice as to an exact figure that should be charged. Every situation is unique, and only you can know what is right for you. Use this book, do the homework, and you won't go wrong.

But before leaving you, I'd like to add one more ingredient to the mix. You must believe in yourself and your own worth. You wouldn't have started your own business if you didn't have a strong measure of this, and now that I've given you insight into the psychology and art of fee-setting, I want you to go out there with confidence. Once you've determined what a fair rate will be, there's no need to bid low or to bid apologetically. *You know you're worth it.* Now express that confidence, and you'll start getting the fees you deserve!

XVII. APPENDIX

THE BASICS OF A LETTER OF AGREEMENT

A basic letter of agreement will contain:

- What will you provide?
- When are the services or the product to be delivered?
- What will the client provide?
- Are there any special terms to be specified?
- What is the fee and when is it to be paid?
- What expenses are to be reimbursed? When will the expenses be billed and when is that bill due?
- How can this agreement be terminated? (With some types of agreements, you may wish to omit this. However, in some agreements you will want to specify how either party could terminate.)

Additional Tips:

- Type the letter on your own letterhead following a business letter format.

- If the letter runs more than one page, have both parties initial the page(s) they do not sign.

- Check with your local library (or a friend who is a lawyer). They may have books of legal forms which will show additional sample letters of agreement. But remember, you don't have to write in legal-ese.

- DO NOT TRY TO COPY THE FOLLOWING EXAMPLES. The circumstances of your agreements will be different, and you will do better starting from scratch.   To adequately protect yourself, it's important that your letter reflect exactly what *you* need.

CLIENT
Marketing Department
The XYZ Company
333 Fifth Avenue
New York, NY 10028

Dear CLIENT:

This is to confirm our agreement concerning the writing of a brochure tentatively
entitled "Make Your Money Grow With The XYZ Company" which we discussed
at our meeting on October 19.

I will write a 1000-word sales brochure on this topic which will be delivered to
you prior to November 15. Two re-writes, based on your comments, are included
in this price.

The XYZ Company will provide me with copies of old sales literature as well as
new material concerning the direction this brochure should take. If I should need
any additional material, the Marketing Department will either provide me with
the research I need or give me direct access to the person who can answer my
questions.

For this work, I will be paid $1000.00. The first installment of the fee will be
$330 and is payable by November 1, with return of this letter, which is to be
signed by you. The remaining $670 will be paid within 30 days of delivery.

Please sign and return this agreement. I look forward to working with you.

Sincerely,

Independent Contractor

                                        Accepted by:

                                        _____
                                        for the XYZ Company

                                        Date_____

CLIENT
DEF Hotel
10298 Wilshire Blvd.
Los Angeles, CA 90204

Dear CLIENT:

As we discussed at our meeting on March 12, The DEF Hotel has identified the
need for better employee communication in order to enhance the company's
overall image.

We have agreed that I shall currently undertake Stage One (The Planning Study)
of the total program we discussed. During the period of the next three months,
I will explore and identify the following:

1.What kind of employee communications tool will be most effective with the
hotel support staff? My report on the subject will be delivered on April 21.

2.What kind of communications tool will be most effective with the managerial
staff? My report on this subject will be delivered May 5.

3.How can the employee communications program at DEF's new property, the
GHI Hotel in Phoenix (which already has a program in place) be improved? This
report will be delivered by June 5.

The DEF Hotel will provide me with office space at both hotel locations and
complete secretarial phone coverage throughout the duration of these studies.
Unlimited access to personnel will also be granted.

My fee for the work described will be $3500; $1000 payable on March 26; $1250
payable on May 5; and the remaining $1250 payable by June 30.

The DEF Hotel will reimburse me for long-distance phone calls and for all
travel-related expenses including air fare and out-of-pocket expenses, however,
the out-of-pocket expenses will not exceed $30 without the approval of CLIENT.
A room and meals at the GHI Hotel will also be provided for the duration of my
stay. Expenses will be billed monthly and are payable within 30 days. Additional
services beyond the scope of this project will be charged on a per day basis at
the rate of $300 per day, with the minimum being $150 for a half-day.

Should the DEF Hotel abandon this project, I must be notified by April 10. It is
understood that I shall be entitled to retain or collect any and all fees and
reimbursements due me on April 10. In the event that The DEF Hotel does not

notify me in a timely fashion of its intent to terminate, my total fee of $3500 shall be considered due and payable.

If for whatever reason I am unable to complete the Planning Study, I shall give written notice of same to The DEF Hotel within 15 days of the delivery date of the next report. I shall deliver any reports due before that date and collect any and all amounts due me through the date of termination.

If at the conclusion of the Planning Study, The DEF Hotel wishes to retain me to implement the suggestions which come as a result of these studies, we will discuss a new agreement at that time.

Please initial page one of this agreement and sign below before returning this agreement.

Sincerely,

Independent Contractor

                                        Accepted by:

                                        _____
                                        for The DEF Hotel

                                        _____
                                        Date

COLLEGE COUNSELING FOR THE GHI SCHOOL

Independent Contractor's Services and Fees

Specific services I will provide:

1. Meet individually with college-bound junior and seniors to outline their college options. Provide each with a list of appropriate colleges and clear directions on how to obtain applications and information. Help students fill out applications.

2. Write letters of recommendation for students applying to private colleges, and petition letters to support public university candidates.

3. Meet weekly with the senior class in the fall to discuss testing, meeting application deadlines, narrowing their college lists, writing application essays.

4. Represent the GHI School at appropriate professional meetings and conferences.

5. Provide GHI parents with timely, accurate information about college choice and admission testing, financial aid, etc. This includes offering a College Night for parents, writing a column for the GHI newsletter, and meeting with parents at the School at their request.

6. Update the GHI College Handbook as necessary.

Schedule of payment for services:

Payment of $1100.00 per month, starting October 1, 199-, over nine months (final payment on June 1, 199-).

It is to be understood by GHI School that I am not responsible for the following:

1. Test registration: Ordering CEEB materials, administering tests, processing registrations.

2. Processing applications Collecting fees, reminding students to fill out applications, asking teachers to write recommendations.

3. Preparing transcripts for colleges and calculating grade point average.

4. Maintaining files of college information, coordinating and taking notes on visits of admission deans to GHI, ordering books and catalogues.

GHI agrees to perform the above duties on a timely basis, in order for me to be able to fulfill this contract.

_____
Independent Contractor

Agreed to by:

_____
Director, GHI School

Date_____

CLIENT
Marketing Services Manager
JKL, Inc.
1515 Winter St.
Larchmont, NY 10538

Dear CLIENT:

It was good to see you again. As discussed, we are sending you this letter to confirm our agreement on the design of a symbol and/or logo type for JKL, Inc.

1.Basing our work on what we've discussed along with a review of competitors' identifications, MNY Associates will develop at least eight rough sketches of possible symbols and/or logo types.

2.We will develop a more finished sketch from the most successful candidate.

3.We will also develop and recommend in written form other basic elements of a design system. This would include compatible type styles, color palette, etc.

4.We will design a business card which would demonstrate the appropriateness and flexibility of the basic elements of your system.

Schedule of Fees and Expenses

Design exploration	$1500.00
Finished sketch of symbol and/or logo type	$ 300.00
Design and comprehensive for cards	$ 150.00
Typography and expenses (estimated)	$ 200.00
Total	$2150.00

Expenses

If the expenses are likely to run over the $200 estimate, the additional expenditure will have prior authorization from JKL, Inc.

Additional Services

Additional services performed outside the scope of this project will be charged on a time and material basis. Our rates for design are $70 per hour and $45 for production.

Schedule

Three weeks from authorization.

We'll look forward to hearing from you.

Sincerely,

Independent Contractor

Accepted by _____
                          JKL, Inc.

Date_____

This letter provides a boilerplate letter of agreement for a company which performs a specific service on an hourly basis. When performing a similar service for many clients (as opposed to varying services for a few clients), then an all-purpose letter such as this one makes a lot of sense. Note that full name, address, and phone number of the client is requested. This makes both performance of the service and/or collection easier in a case where many clients are likely involved.

Agreement to Provide Services

This is to confirm that you have hired STU Company for the purpose of:

STU rates will be $_____per hour for the time spent on the assignment. Client also agrees to pay out-of-pocket expenses incurred by STU in performing the required work.

STU is hereby authorized to spend up to _____hours on the project and $_____amount may be spent on reasonable expenses. These limits shall not be exceeded without authorization from the client.

Client agrees to pay $_____as a non-refundable advance. The balance remaining will be due and payable within 30 days or completion of the project.

Work will not commence until STU has received a signed copy of this document along with the agreed-upon deposit.

Signed:_____
                STU Company

Agreed to by:

_____
Client

_____
Address

_____
City, State, Zip

_____
Phone Number

Here's a sample of a consultant's price list, including terms and conditions:

Schedule of Consultation Fees

DAILY RATES

$1,000 per day. Minimum billing: half-day.

WEEKLY/MONTHLY RATES

Weekly/monthly contracts are available. The fees are calculated at the daily rate, based on five-day weeks and 20-day months.

TERMS AND CONDITIONS

Daily fees are due and payable upon receipt of Consultant's invoice.

Weekly/monthly engagements must be initiated by purchase order or letter of agreement, specifying responsibilities of both parties.

Weekly/monthly fees are due and payable on the day immediately prior to the first day of the engagement.

Each staff person of Consultant keeps a log of all time spent on a specific engagement. That log will be made available for inspection by the client, at the client's request.

"Out-of-pocket" expenses incurred by Consultant on behalf of the Client will be documented and billed to the Client at cost. These expenses will generally, but not exclusively, cover: transportation, rooms, meals, auto rentals, long-distance telephone charges, etc.

Expenses are due and payable on receipt of Consultant's invoice.

RETAINER CONTRACTS

Following any engagement, Consultant may be retained to provide professional continuity. This allows client response on a "first priority" basis. As each situation is unique, retainer contracts will be quoted at specific request of a client.

Client _Jones & Co._   Due Date _4-14_

Phone _213-555-0602_

Address _10701 Flower_   Agreed Upon Fee _$750.00 + expenses_

Los Angeles, CA 90024   Deposit _$200.00_

Project _Sales Booklet - needs immediately; agreed to one re-write_

Date	Start	Stop	Daily Total	Work Accomplished
3-28	9:30 A	10:00 A	1/2 hour	Discussed info w/ Mr. Jones
3-29	10:00 A	12:00 N	2 hrs.	Planned & made notes
4-2	10:00 A	1:00 P	3 hrs.	Wrote first draft/checked w/ Jones
4-3	9:00 A	2:00 P	5 hrs.	Rewrote final copy
4-7	12:00 N	5:00 P	5 hrs.	Worked in changes - rewrote final copy

Total: _15 1/2 hrs._

Date	Expenditures	Amount
3-28	L.A. phone call - 22 min.	$6.40
4-2	L.A. phone call - 20 min.	$5.90
4-3	Air Express	$15.00
4-8	Air Express	$15.00

Total: _$42.30_

Notes
follow-up in July to see if they want to go forward with employee manual.

Client _____ Due Date _____

Phone _____

Address _____ Agreed Upon Fee _____

_____ Deposit _____

Project _____

Date	Start	Stop	Daily Total	Work Accomplished

Total:_____

Notes

Date	Expenditures	Amount

_____
_____
_____
_____
_____
_____

Total:_____